PRATEEK KUMAR

A Day can change your life

Master of the day

POWERFUL REPEATABLE CUSTOMIZABLE FRAMEWORK BASED ON UNIVERSAL PRINCIPLES TO MASTER YOUR DAY AND LIFE

ISBN: 978-9948-35-775-9

Acknowledgments

This book is dedicated to my parents who made me what I am. They are no longer with me but continue to surround me with their inspiration. From them, the mantle was taken over by my wife who leaves no stone unturned in making space for all my pursuits. I would like to thank her for all the support and help she provided me to complete the book. I would like to thank my elder son, Siddhant, who suggested many important changes and painstakingly picked bloopers from my half-baked drafts. While my younger son, Rishaan, though very young, gave some stunning insights which we the "rational" adults miss out in our straitjacketed existence.

On the professional side, I would like to thank Vanessa Mendozzi, with whom I had the good fortune of meeting online. She is the creative spirit behind the cover and the overall layout. She not only has given this manuscript the professional edge but has also patiently put up with all the incessant changes that I suggested and turned them into polished outputs in double-quick time.

Apart from this, I would like all my team members, colleagues, relations and friends who provided invaluable feedback on this topic and have cheered each piece that I wrote on any fora and made me look extraordinarily good. It's their encouragement and generous praise that made me believe that I can extend my writing streak further.

While I embark on this pursuit to act as a bridge to bring corporate quality philosophies into our daily life, I would like to thank all my colleagues in various organizations that I worked for in the past 25 years and the numerous client organizations that I had the honor to contribute to making their businesses a little better. This book wouldn't have been possible without the learning that each person I got associated with gave me. Let's begin without much further ado.

About the Author

Prateek is a Quality and Business Excellence expert and preacher. He is a practicing Lean Thinker and a Master Black Belt in Six Sigma. Based out of Dubai, he works with some of the biggest names on the business firmament in the Banking, Retail and IT sectors in the Middle East in helping take their business processes towards excellence. He has been working for the last 25 years' in the quality domain for organizations like IBM, LG Electronics and several other reputed companies in India. In the process, he has worked agnostic of the domains for big global clients spread across Banking, Retail, IT, Telecom and Healthcare verticals. His belief is that all the underlying philosophies behind the quality and business process improvement methodologies are universal and are equally applicable in our personal life. His avowed interest and passion is to apply these core underlying principles governing these methods like Lean, Six Sigma, Process re-engineering to improve human potential in the age of disruption that we are currently in.

He is a vociferous reader, speaker and writes extensively across various mediums including his blog, MasteroftheDay.com / Prateeklive.com on topics such as Technology, Time IQ, Lean, Life and Nostalgia.

Contents

THE AWAKENING

THE EXECUTION

THE EVOLUTION

A Note to the Reader

Time is just a man-made measure of our existence on earth. There is nothing like time in nature. Before we were born or after we die, nothing exists. It's beyond our consciousness. While we are alive, we have a thousand things to do, experience, obtain and also provide but our existence is finite and from the moment we were born, its depletion starts, but we continue without realizing that it will end one day. The end of our existence on earth will be a one-time event and we are still to reach it. It is thus pertinent to realize this one absolute truth that we can only do and live just that much. Within that space exists time and we can utilize it the way we want. Thus time is a precious resource, in whatever way we look at it. Whatever we may aspire for in terms of riches, creativity, relationships or anything else can be had sooner if we better plan our existence.

At the same time, what we have before us is only the present moment or at most the day in front of us. Yesterday has already lapsed. Tomorrow may or may not come. But we continue as if tomorrow is a certainty and there will be an infinite number of them. Even if we assume, without sounding ominous that average human life expectancy is say 75 years, the variation is something we can never be sure of. The statistical average score is not a good determinant of age at an individual level. At the same time, we age as we go along, thus, no longer is our body that efficient in the last phase of our life, nor do we have the energy and vigour to be able to do what we can in our youth. Thus, things have to be done in a timely way so we can pace our life accordingly.

There is a swarm of time management books out there to tell you a few anecdotes, give some steps and few handy tips that together are supposed to turn you into a "time management and productivity champion". However, their lack of a cohesive approach is apparent as we fail to understand as to how to convert those words into action or how to remember the trivia presented in a non-coherent sequence. They are pieces of loosely strung together concepts which might teach a trick to do your work faster but the fact is that life is not just about a bag of tricks. You're in it every second of it. Clearly, random concepts and euphuisms alone will not do. What is needed is a repeatable and practical framework that one can employ to become more effective within the space that a day offers all of us.

I have been in the domain of quality management and business excellence all my working life so far having practiced and witnessed the advent and decline of various quality management philosophies and methodologies over the past twenty-five years; While Deming and Juran laid the foundations of modern quality management, the Japanese turned it into an art. Introducing techniques like ISO-9000 made the adoption of basic tenets of quality management universal. Six Sigma introduced a systematic way of problem-solving using statistics while *Lean Thinking* provided a philosophy of looking at work from a waste, balancing and pulls perspective. All these quality techniques are based on universal philosophies that are applicable not just to industrial or services processes but to our personal life as well. In our actual life also we follow processes, good or bad, fast or slow. We all have certain behavioral patterns that we repeat daily without even being aware of it. Our life is a sum total of those repetitions to a large extent. We act in certain ways that are unique to us. Only by close observation or by comparison with others can we discern how our routine, behavior and work methods differ. The good part is that we can change and get rid of unproductive patterns if we concertedly focus on eliminating them. But, it requires a repeatable approach for developing and habituating patterns that overwrite the previous ones.

I saw a big dichotomy in being a preacher of quality and lean thinking in professional life to some of the biggest corporate clients globally and then being so disorganized in my real life. Clearly, I was not walking the talk or I was not seeing my two selves as one holistic whole. My daily routine would remain largely disorganized, driven by events and occurrences which were a heady mix of lack of planning and anticipation, bad habits, never-ending procrastination and keeping professional work as a priority at all costs. Thus my days would be a largely a shapeless mass driven by "official tasks and projects of the day", no fixed time for doing anything, little physical activity, no distinction between office and personal space and many other things which characterize perhaps a lot of us to one extent or the other.

I made attempts on and off to include a few good habits, daily time routines, better-eating habits, and physical activity. And, yes, of course, reading scores of self-improvement books. But, nothing worked. This made me deeply disturbed and restless. I had the "Best in Class" tools applicable universally but I was not much different from an average person having no knowledge of these principles. I reckoned that if I were to apply these principles in daily life, then they should propel me and by corollary, anyone else also to function more efficiently. Thus started the quest to distill the concepts that I tested in live working scenarios and also side by side kept documenting and refining them. I began to inculcate and test these principles in my daily life to manage my time better. Along the journey, I tried a number of approaches based on these principles. Some worked some didn't. I also learnt a few startling facts and principles which if violated will ensure failure or suboptimal results in whatever we may do. I am sure that you will also create a more customized version for yourself once you adopt the practices outlined in the book. This book is a living and breathing manual that will evolve as you learn to manage yourself during the day in progressively better ways.

This book takes you through a never before approach using a framework and a self-tested process to ensure that we do things that matter and still leave us time to enjoy life. This book is meant for anyone who wants to take control of their life one day at a time. This is not a one size prescription for anyone and everyone. Rather, it is a framework that you can use to organize your day and in fact your entire life.

My hypothesis was that if it can work for an ordinary person like me, then it can work for anyone! I treated myself as the guinea pig and implemented them myself. You can do this too. If you want to make a difference in your life, the place to start is the day that is just arriving shortly. Get ready to change your life!

As the book evolved, my objectives were to keep things simple for anyone to adopt these principles for better self-management without even being aware of the origins of the concepts and practices which lie at the heart of the methodology that you are about to learn.

This book contrary to your view is not only about doing more within the time you have or do it faster but it is about creating the space and cut out the noise that surrounds and keeps us stressed out. You deserve to enjoy your life while it is there. It is about doing things efficiently that you need to do to lead a stress-free life in this civilized world.

We keep ourselves tangled in small time tasks and activities losing sight of our goals or the balance that is so essential and before we know, a phase of our life is over. Nothing is more frustrating than realizing that a part of our life has gone by without our dreams fulfilled and doing what we always wanted to do.

After having trained hundreds of professionals on the concept of Quality, Lean, Re-engineering and Six-Sigma, this is a unique take on time management and introduces the same quality principles in managing ourselves to utilize the day as a unit of our life.

A day cannot and should not be wasted. That's all we have right now! You can't let it wander in the past or be worried excessively about the future. Yesterday is a lesson, tomorrow could be the outcome of what we do today. So, let's focus on what we could achieve today.

If you are like millions of others who also struggle with your day and want to explore how to make it count, then the time has come. It may not be a perfect prescription for all that may be going wrong in your life, but at the end of it, it will equip you with the approach to control your day and handle your other issues in a much better frame of mind.

The steps outlined in the following pages can change your life if you want. It's the result of painstakingly observing how we go about our daily life, what is it that high performers do differently and why despite all our best intentions we don't seem to be able to get started and keep whirring our wheels at the same spot without moving forward. If you follow the steps, it will work for each one of you who will go through it. It cuts out the fluff and quickly provides a methodology to adopt in your daily routine. Having said that, the book only provides a framework; it's up to you on how to customize it to meet your needs and circumstances.

Initially, you may find the ideas presented in the book to be too elaborate to be followed. But be assured nothing worthwhile in life comes easy. Things won't change all of a sudden. You yourself will be resisting what the change entails. Initially, nothing much may happen, but if your decide and persist then surely you will evolve your own design on how you want to lead your life from now on and get a sense of balance that you never had before.

You got to walk that extra mile towards success. Remember

the time you started to learn how to drive. It seemed daunting and complex. Many years later, you don't even have to think about the rules and controls while driving.

Ask yourself the question that have you decided to take hold of your life and turn it into something meaningful? Are you ready to make that change that will make you a better and happier person overall? If you find the answer is an emphatic "Yes", then be ready to make the sacrifices required to take your goals towards a heady climax and conclusion. It's not a miracle book or one that gives you a magic formula to tame time or suddenly turn you into a performance champion. It just provides you a perspective, framework and a set of practices on time management and lets you develop what works best for you. Its concepts may work for you fully or partially but they will. Some will very soon become a part of your life. Some will not. The idea is to liberate and not tie you down to a set of rituals.

You may get overwhelmed if you take on everything at one go. Thus, switch to what you can adopt and adapt to gradually. Like any other framework, it has to be tuned and customized to your requirements. Go on and customize as much as you want. The idea is to help you organize your life one day at a time without losing sight of your dreams, goals, and aspirations.

This book is meant for?

Everyone will benefit from this book. It provides a malleable and extendable framework that applies to everyone's life. It might be useful differently to different readers. An office executive or manager may find this much more useful to structure their day compared to a worker in a factory or a salesman at a shop whose day and duties are fixed. However, the book has something for everyone. It will give you ideas and suggestions to rethink your daily routine and your life in general. Ultimately, this book is for anyone and everyone who wants to lead a better life, a day at a time.

But before beginning the book, start believing in the hypothesis, *"A day is enough to change your life!"*

THE AWAKENING

A Day to do it

"The future starts today, not tomorrow"
Pope John Paul II

1.1 IS TIME FOR REAL?

It's very interesting to get a perspective of what "time" is to understand further how to manage it. Everyone has a favorite excuse for delaying taking action by saying, "I wish I could do it but don't have time. But, is time for real or we should say instead "I wish I could do it but am too disorganized to do it".

Nature has its own rhythm and soon the sun resplendent in the sky goes down the horizon and the light has ended. Darkness falls! Time today is meant to track our existence on earth and tell us when the day will start and when night will descend. During the day the concept of an hour, minute and seconds is meant to enable happening of man-made events at the set time of the day or night.

Thousands of years back, however, there was no concept of time. Various civilizations have tried to track the alternate light and dark and the cold or warm periods that enveloped them periodically. To understand and predict when exactly light would change into darkness and vice versa, man looked at the source i.e. the sun and the moon. Day and night were not defined till then and were considered to be opposites of each other rather than being part of a day. Markets and work activities started with the sunrise and continued either till noon or till darkness fell.

Apart from this, when seasons changed, man could see that the sun has again changed position and they felt hot or cold depending upon what season was setting in. However, one thing was certain that there was a periodicity to all these events which led to its tracking.

Initial tracking of time was based on the length of the shadows that objects placed on the ground would cast depending upon the position of the sun. These were referred to as Sun-dials. These gadgets only worked if the sky was not cloudy. Thus, man kept looking for ways to design alternative devices not dependent on celestial bodies. This led to the creation of water clocks, sand glass and even incenses sticks to track time. Sundials and water clocks had markings to show the passage of time which eventually led dark and light periods being divided into 12 parts and which further solidified the concept of a 24-hour day.

However, it wasn't until the Greek astronomer Hipparchus propounded that both day time and night time was divided into 12 hours of 60 minutes each that the actual contours of the division of the day were laid out. The Greeks also divided each degree of the 360 degrees in a circle into 60 smaller parts. This division came to be known as minutes and each of these 60 minutes were further divided into 60 parts, which came to be known as seconds. This laid the foundation of time management as we know today.

Calendars were initially based on the moon and later, on the sun movement. Pope Gregory XIII introduced the Gregorian calendar which was only gradually over a period of several hundred years accepted across the world. It is now the most widely used calendar worldwide.

In 1884, American President Chester A. Arthur organized the International Meridian Conference to have a common reference point based on which the clocks around the world could be set. Greenwich was chosen as the prime meridian which indicates zero-degree longitude. Time across the world can be understood with reference to the Greenwich Mean Time (GMT).

Thus, time doesn't have any meaning until we put all these discoveries and concepts of time measurement devices, calendars and time units into it. From sunrise to sunset is what we have to work and beyond that, we take a break till the next day dawns when earth revolves enough for us to see the sun again.

1.2 BETWEEN SUNRISE AND SUNSET LIES YOUR SUCCESS STORY

Time passes by, measured by our breaths, or by the length of your shadow,
It came to us like a playful wave as a child, touched us and went away
It came to us like an energetic wind during our youth and took us a distance,
It wrapped around us like a gentle pullover when old, kept us warm
Time will always be there with you, till your time comes!

Every day a new Sun dawns and brings with it the promise of fulfilling our wishes. It has within it potential golden moments of brilliant ideas, fast execution, unbridled laughter, happiness, riches and contentment and can have all that it takes to let us achieve the wildest of our dreams and all that we aspire for. But in reality, days come and days go. They all look the same and turn out to be the same for millions like us. For a minority, though the same time-space creates wealth, happiness, recreation and creativity that we only dream of. While the subject of success covering all aspects of what will make you reach those levels is out of the scope of this discussion, however, what will be discussed is the use of the time-space that we call a day to be equally available to you to focus and succeed at whatever you aspire to do and what brings you happiness and contentment.

Most of us get stuck in a groove that goes on for ages before something different happens. Time flies away, before we know we are old and can't believe that what seems like yesterday happened decades ago. That's the illusion that our mind creates. Days soon add up into months and years and before we know it's time for the final whistle. If you still need proof that the future will arrive way too soon, you only have to look at the time which has gone by. But you can take charge any day you decide and grab the day and start living a much better life matching our dreams and aspirations.

Our life in this world is measured by seconds, minutes hours, day and so on. Anything less than a day can only be measured through an instrument, like a clock. We have been bred on concepts of time which revolve around a clock. A day though can be measured between sunrise and sunset after which the night falls. In olden times when clocks were not invented, people used to get a sense of time through the position of the sun till night fell. Till now we more or less look outside the window to check the progress of the day. We still have some hours before the date changes. The new date starts at 12 AM but we won't be up till about several hours from it. Depending upon your waking up time the work window is open for 9 to 12 hours. This is our window of opportunity. What we do during it will determine whether we are a success or lead an average life as millions live. For many people though, their professions block out this "window of opportunity". They are engaged in work that is fixed and repetitive and require low intellect utilisation.

We all have 24 hours to spend which we call a day. The concept of time management as we are told is based on the premise that time is at our disposal and we are controlling it. However, time is in fact just a frame of reference to define our coordinates in the universe and to respond to events.

How we get a sense of time is through observation. Night

changes into day and back, the cycle of seasons keeps repeating, human beings grow old and are aged based on the number of years they have spent from their birth. It is only in context to the changes happening around us can we actually get a sense of time.

Thus, only a day has any significance for us. Yesterday lives no more. Tomorrow has not yet arrived. All days are the same and add up to form a week, a month, a year, a decade, a century or even longer. We thus spend our time in "day" units which even without a clock we can decipher. For measuring anything smaller we need to have a clock. A second, minute or hour does not have any real significance for us till the time we are in a work scenario where duration is measured in these units like starting of a meeting or a movie show, flight departure time, opening and closing of markets and business establishments etc.

Then why do we need to master our day? The issue is that if we want to achieve anything significant in life these are the only blocks of time at our disposal at any given point of time. For us yesterday has ceased to exist and tomorrow has still not arrived.

But many brilliant talents have withered away because they were not able to exploit their talents and just couldn't do much in life. We all complain about lack of time but the fact is that we are not able to manage ourselves. Time is just a dimension of our existence. Between sunrise and sunset, we have to move forward towards our goal but all that we manage to do is to get a few things accomplished. A few of us within the same constraints put forward by nature are able to progress, prosper and do much more. What do they do differently within the confines of the day that ordinary mortals don't?

Reams of research have been published on this subject and an army of motivational gurus have all the insights that you need to make it to the success league. Strangely, while there is a lot of statistics around how many millions this knowledge has benefitted, virtually very little or none at all is known on how many actually were able to break the shackles of mediocrity and rose to meet their destiny. Anyways, this book is not about the efficacy of these techniques rather this book picks up action in the daily chaos that surrounds us and tries to make a case for an alternative approach to be able to make space for achieving our dreams, becoming more productive and be able to create a daily routine that leaves us invigorated. For this, we will explore the approach and toolkit for you to succeed, do more and be more productive and lead a less stressful life within a day in your life.In fact within a day you are perfectly capable of turning around your complete life.

Whatever may you wish to achieve in life, one thing is for sure that throughout your life, the Sun will continue to rise and set, signalling the end of the day. All your successes, joys, and pains will happen in this frame of reference and nowhere else. Whether there are more successes than defeats, more creativity than listlessness, it's up to you. The way you spend your day is how you will lead your future life.

1.3 IS TIME MANAGEMENT A MISNOMER?

Contrary to what you may think, good time management is not about packing your waking hours with work and more work, rather it is to execute around our priorities, create a balance between work and personal life and make space for rejuvenation. Within this space is where life thrives, the rest of the time we are virtually working like a machine. By tracking time through a clock we think we are being efficient, but are we doing the right set of activities that will take us forward, or make us happier, richer, healthier & better?

Only working and not focusing on other areas of your life like family, self, social, can create an imbalance and ultimately stress. Not working in congruence with what we actually want to do and what we value leads to a state of energy imbalance. The energy lies within us inert and starts acting on us negatively in the form of frustration, desperation, and defeat. Understand, this is your body's way of telling you that the energy must be spent. But why is the energy rarely evident and why only a few are able to capitalize upon it?

The abundance of universal energy that lies within us is not realized by us as we hardly get time in our struggle for daily survival to brood over what we really are and capable of. Years of mediocrity, bad habits and self-perception takes us further and further from reality and make us lead an ordinary life. Thus, when something big comes up we back away swiftly as we cannot handle the pressure that comes along with it. The life of an average person is thus an endless series of opportunities not availed.

1.4 WHAT CAN YOU ACHIEVE IN A DAY?

On an average day if we are not planned or nothing is scheduled, then nothing seems urgent. The mind keeps going back to its steady-state. Take for example what happens over the weekend. There is no pressure to get up, go to work or do any of the activities which happens over a normal work day. Until and unless we have planned for some action, we will not do anything even remotely mimicking a normal week day. Why does this happen?

You might be a student wanting to score big in your final examination or a sportsperson aspiring to win that coveted medal, a corporate manager trying to balance a maddening set of project requirements or a housewife ensuring that the daily chores are finished as quickly as possible so that it leaves her time to pursue an online course or read a book. The circumstances and needs will be different but the fundamentals around making space, becoming more productive, striking a work-life balance or reducing stress will not change. We as human beings will aspire for things that are omnipresent and at our disposal but we create distance from them by tying ourselves up in commitments and deprive ourselves of sunshine, laughter, relaxation and many other things in life which are all around us but we only cast a fleeting glance at them and then pay for a holiday to return to nature. Thus it is also very important to reset our priorities, values and what we consider as important in our lives to be able to take out time to just connect back to life.

We may know our mind but, our heart is an unpredictable character. It makes us do what may not be appropriate but it keeps us safe in a state of minimum energy. Doing anything else would mean that this basal energy state will rise. Therein lays a universal secret! We must be ready to raise our energy by following a series of steps to achieve a small task or a big goal. These steps are a part of all the work that we do. Some of them may not be required but these fundamental steps can't be ignored. We will look at these steps in detail in the following chapters. We have within the day multiple opportunities to do what we strive for but we must plan for them to be included. Some basic goals that we all have includes a desire to be healthier, better, happier and richer. All these goals can be achieved but we have to create space for them and have to be persisted with. The reason why it works is that you are reading the book which came through by following this philosophy.

We know that we can achieve all this but still, we find ourselves wasting a major part of the day knowing fully well that time is getting wasted without considering what all we are missing by being in this state of ambivalence. The good news is that right now, at this very moment you can take specific actions to begin this journey. Ultimately there are no real grand designs or goals to be achieved at an unspecified time in the future. The future doesn't exist right now all you have is the present day in front of you. Even if you reach that point of time when you have time to spare to begin what you want to do, it is your today where you can sow the seeds for making this a reality.

1.5 THE NEED TO BECOME THE MASTER OF THE DAY

Have you ever expressed these frustrations?

- "I don't know where my days go"," There are so many things I never seem to have time to do…"
- "I find it difficult to switch off even after coming back from work"

- "I never seem to have time for my spouse and children"
- "I never seem to get started on life changing projects even when I have the capability to achieve all of them"

All these reactions are very normal and we all face them. In fact, considering the complexities of modern day life and based on what you are out to achieve, we will inevitably be faced with these situations.

Just as we age from childhood to old age, we go through our day waking up fresh and lively as a child and then slowly we progress through the afternoon like middle age and finally we are done at the end of the day which is akin to old age and finally we fall asleep. This is like dying, albeit it's a temporary death as we get up the next morning and get another lease of life. But the most important point to note is that whatever life stage that is over will not come back. Similarly, a day gone by will never come back. Yesterday is just a memory.

A day is a microcosm of our life. In a day we can take decisions and actions which can sow the seeds for future happiness. The way we spend our day usually is the way we end up spending our life. If you look back you will see rows upon rows of yesterdays filled with usual stuff except for the days on which something special happened. This will keep on happening till the time we start doing something that leads us to do something else, a change of business, job, location, an event or anything that changes the course of your life. It may even be something smaller like planning a holiday, throwing a celebration bash, achieving a sales target, making an investment or anything else that made you happier, healthier, better or richer. You will notice, however, that one thing in common amongst all the events listed above is that you make them happen when you planned for it and go through the grind before the goal is achieved. You have to go through the cycle of planning for the goal, undertake the actions involved, sacrifice in various ways, and finally reach the climax when the goal is achieved. The pace of action will pick up and you will be filled with unbridled energy and that is when the moment will come when finally the goal is finally achieved. Also, note one thing that all this happens in a fairly short period of time. There will be days nearing completion when you have your hands full, you will make quick decisions and move quickly. Whatever you do will add value and you will make incremental progress. Notice that the value added actions takes a minuscule amount of time compared to the weeks or months that might have been taken just to get started or to reach a decision.

But unfortunately, such days and periods are far in-between. Our days generally are an uncontrolled phenomenon with lots happening around and a lot that we would like to do and control.

Unfortunately, the plethora of time management tools like diaries, calendars, scheduling apps, and software available using which we can "program" our day and through these keep a tab through timely reminders alarms, buzzers, and notifications to alert you also have a limited utility. They can help plan for the "normal" days but when it comes to the days when there are a dozen different priorities and multiple pulls then all these tools are forgotten. Only a framework in which you can make quick changeovers, manage distractions and be at your productive best can help you cope with the variety that life throws at us when we endeavor to reach beyond our boundaries

But you may be asking "Why I have to adapt to these elaborate arrangements when there are other people who know nothing about this but still are much more successful and prosperous". There is no easy answer. They have may have more resolve, focus, drive, money, resources, connections or whatever but could still struggle to lead a balanced life. You will never know. But one thing that you know for sure is how you are leading your life. Every moment of your life is under the control of the choices you are making, positive or negative.

To give up on your dreams is to put a spoke in the wheels of the universal intelligence you possess and which was sent on earth with a definite purpose. You can't peep into others brains. You are looking for answers to set a few things in your life in order and hence reading this book. Give it a try!

The famous Japanese poem, Iroha, written in the Heian era (794–1179) beautifully sums up our life in a few lines and encapsulates the undeniable truth of life that we are going towards a definite end. It goes something like this,

Although its scent still lingers on, the form of a flower has scattered away
For whom will the glory of this world remain unchanged?
Arriving today at the yonder side of the deep mountains of evanescent existence
We shall never allow ourselves to drift away intoxicated, in the world of shallow dreams.

Our life is finite. It is foolish to allow any negativity to seep into your life. It's like burning in the fire which you only can kindle and keep stoking.

To master our day is the first step towards mastering our life. You have no other option as we are presented life only a day at a time.

1.6 ARE YOU READY TO MASTER YOUR DAY?

We are in our own special way nothing less than supercomputers. We are the product of the energy that pervades the universe and have an evolved brain which can dream and also manifest the dream into reality. In us, we constitute one complete unit of the universe.

I am reminded of a story I heard once about how baby elephants when brought to a circus for training are initially tied to a strong pole after a training session. The young baby elephants not used to being tied try to break free frantically for several days. They remain unsuccessful! Slowly, their efforts become feeble and they reconcile to the fact that when tied with a rope around their neck, it's futile to break free. This soon turns into behavior which carries on till their adult life. The elephants are sometimes tied to a mere peg with a rope. A peg doesn't have the strength to withstand the immense power of a giant and powerful animal but the strength of the mind conditioning their mind have received over many years since childhood ensures that all the might that the elephant possesses is slave to that mental weakness and it never tries to break free even though all it will take them is one strong pull to break free. We humans also are like those elephants, life brings us down so much that even though it might just take one single pull to break free but we never try to break that proverbial peg of conditioning that keeps us from attaining personal freedom and success.

We are much behind what we could achieve in totality if everyone realizes their potential. The entire worldwide education and work system breeds mediocrity and pays a pittance for the services rendered to a majority of people. We have already lost hundreds of years of cumulative human excellence due to a servile environment and self-limiting thoughts induced by it.

Every now and then we have flashes of brilliance in the world's professions and we are overawed by our own aura. But, instead of being dazzled we must realize that this is what we are in each one of us in essence. When subjected to a force, the real self comes out and helps us achieve feats which in our inertial state is difficult to visualize. The energy within us has to be subjected to a force to give it acceleration. With this knowledge, approach each day as if nothing can stop you except your own lack of confidence. You may have lost your confidence somewhere down negotiating life twists and turns and let your personality suffer and get suppressed. This is the biggest gift you can give yourself and to the entire mankind perhaps.

The prognosis of our underachievement lies in the way we plan and execute our day. You will find in the day of a common man are vast expanses of non-value added tasks and wasted time which will never contribute to any sort of success. This type of routine does not create any challenge, prosperity or happiness. But we carry on and keep on doing the same things again tomorrow. We have psychologically given up like these baby elephants and have stopped the effort to break free. But the fact remains that we have all the strength to get whatever we dream to achieve.

A day is about to dawn. You can make yourself richer, healthier, better, happier and all that you wish. At the same time, you can make yourself inactive, despondent and ill both physically and mentally. The choice is all yours. However, to utilize a day is easier said than done. Until we have decided upon what we will do, know exactly what needs to be done and it and when to do it, we may never get started.

The seeds of a great tomorrow are sown right here, today. Tomorrow will come soon, you will then have no time to brood over things, begin planning, look for stuff, and make decisions. It's too late! A day is meant for pure execution. If you do some or all of the above, then your day is as good as gone. You will procrastinate, leave work incomplete, and forget important tasks. The "Master of the Day" is like a chess player who has the strategy laid out. He or she goes and plays the game to a plan, builds it up and moves in for the kill.

In the next chapter, we will see what we do in our day and why we are driven the way we are. We will also analyze how at a high level we spend our day and create a baseline from where we will begin our pursuit to master our day.

How do we spend the day?

"Either you run the day or the day runs you"
Jim Rohn

2.1 INTRODUCTION

Designing a day is not just about planning activities, but it involves managing a number of elements that you will read about in the coming chapters which play an important part in deciding whether any efforts that we put to accomplish a task is successful or not. While, one may argue that there could be many other factors that play maybe an equal if not greater part in determining success, but I believe that other possible factors like sincerity, dedication, discipline get evoked by systematic identification and management of these factors.

However, the present chapter focuses on elements which

sabotage our day and our success overall. The chapter discusses many of the factors which are not apparent but play an important part in determining whether we even pick up a long cherished goal and if we do then are we successful in sustaining it and taking it to completion. It takes into account the hidden elements which impede any worthwhile endeavor and have to be successfully managed.

2.2 WHAT DO WE ACTUALLY DO IN A DAY?

Do we know how we spend our day? Chances are that if you start recording your daily activities for the next ten days, you will be startled by the amount of time that was spent on inconsequential activities, spending an inordinately long time on simple tasks and time taken away from you by others. If we really want to know and how we can control our day then understanding your daily patterns, activities and time wasters is a great way to get control of our day, boost your productivity and just about everything else in your life. We will discuss here the way to analyze how we spend the day and where exactly are we spending our time on.

We have within a day a variety of activities from the time we wake up. We attend to biological needs, groom ourselves, eat and then become ready to start our workday. The work nature will then determine how we will spend our day from thereon till the evening when we again undergo a changeover and crawl back into our personal space.

The trades of the world are one too many. People on earth are engaged in various professions some dating back to thousands of years and some which have come into existence in the recent past and more are being added every day. The working world today is divided based on the industry. Each of these industries have a vast range of core and ancillary industries associated with them and with thousands of people working in them. Some of these are Manufacturing, Construction, Food, Shipping, Surface Transportation, Aerospace, IT, Chemical, Pharmaceuticals, Education, Medicine, Consumer Goods, Education, Entertainment, Mass media, Energy, Earth excavation industries and many more. These may be in the form of private or government organizations in the form of factories, corporates, retail outlets and various other ancillary businesses associated with them.

People who are employed in either of these sectors have a variety of roles to play at various levels and are accordingly paid. Each sector has its own way set of work, shift system, and people learn the skills through training and experience. But the work rules across remains the same with 8 to 9 hours of our peak time dedicated to the employer. If you are in business you may be working even harder.

Being employed for someone means that you have agreed to dedicate your work, effort and time to your employer organization based upon which you would be compensated. Along with our work we also have to take care of our family, self and various other things that living in a city throws upon us. This brings to us a complex set of requirements to be managed on a daily basis for which we are not trained and no educational system till date caters to it. Since no one stresses upon it, we assume that it is simple and everyone have their own rituals, practices to make sense of it. However, this is the very essence of our daily survival and it's upon us to improve it and not let it overpower you.

A typical day is a mix of activities which we do for a job or business, meeting self and family needs and also spend some time socially. Work comes in all shapes and sizes and can be classified based on various criteria. At a very basic level, it can be divided based upon its complexity, steps involved and duration. These are generally referred to as tasks and projects.

Tasks are a type of work which consists of one or more activities of usually a small duration aimed at achieving an outcome. You are feeling thirsty and pour water into a glass and drink it. Your thirst is satiated. The task is finished! You want to make an online payment and logged into your online banking account, key in the beneficiary details, make the fund transfer and log out. The task is finished. In a day, knowingly or unknowingly, we are doing tens of such tasks. It is the choice of tasks and your ability to keep them in memory which determines if your tomorrow will be better than today or not.

Projects involve one or many people to come together to contribute towards achieving an outcome which could consist of multiple sequential (and some parallel) smaller tasks, each requiring a certain skill and effort. Projects are a type of work which consists of a series of tasks of varying duration leading to an intended outcome. Sometimes they are so long that they have to be broken into a number of sub-projects. Projects require time, resources and have many tasks that have external dependencies and constraints.

Some examples of personal projects are, buying a new house,

searching and landing a new job, starting a business, planning and taking a vacation etc. Examples of corporate or public projects can be like a business set-up or expansion, construction and infrastructure projects, software implementation projects etc.

Depending upon our work nature, our time might be totally tied up requiring dedicated attention like a worker working on a machine or blocked from morning till evening in case of an office job. The office jobs vary from data processing; administration to management and their daily official routine also varies. It may also be a highly skilled job requiring intermittent work periods like a doctor at an OPD, a surgeon performing a surgery or flexible like a manager whose job is to ensure that work is taken from a set of individuals in a team by influencing and managing them to achieve specified organizational objectives.

Thus, we can see our work time is pretty much tied up depending upon our profession and the choices we have made. But the fact remains, we are still human beings. We still have our needs, aspirations, and family to look after. If a major chunk of our day is taken away by work, then the other spheres of our life will suffer until we find some way to strike a balance.

It is very important thus, we evolve some sort of a daily self-management routine to ensure that we are able to achieve all that we aspire to and at the same time not compromise on the other important aspects of our life. We must clarify what we value in life, what we are good at and a set of principles, values and work practices that will keep us healthier, happier, better and richer.

2.3 WHERE DOES YOUR TIME GO?

We have all heard the proverb that "Time Is Money". If time indeed has value then many of us are guilty of spending a bulk of it on virtually nothing! You can, however, correlate that successful people will invariably utilize their time better or in a more productive way. What do they do differently having been given the same amount of time as everyone else? It has got to do with what we do repeatedly day in and day out for years together. Secondly, successful people's workday is filled with activities that a common person may find daunting. There routine consist of taking decisions on the fly, being in public glare, taking risks knowingly or being pushed into situations, they learn to stay outside their comfort zone daily. This is a universal law that to succeed you have to face adversity and pass through it head-on. On the other side of adversity is freedom!

Time is a man-made unit to track our existence. Let's count the day in seconds, all 86400 of it, and say it has a monetary value but unlike money, the unspent time will not be retained. You can use it the way you like but you can't hoard it. It will vanish at the end of the day. This is where the irony lies we spend something as precious as the time that is finite and we use it to earn another quantity called money which gets depleted only when we spend it and left as it is, it will last beyond our lifetime. We may use this time doing nothing or indulging in our passion, feeling happy or swamping ourselves in self-pity. The choice is ours.

It is an established fact that until we have planned our day, we are likely to waste a bulk of our time and energy doing irrelevant things or doing nothing at all. Your rational mind tells you to finish important tasks but your sub-conscious mind has other ideas. We are likely to waste up to 95% of our time and energy during the day doing irrelevant, non-worthwhile things which will not make us healthier, better, happier and richer.

During the day we are being governed by small repetitive rituals, processes, habits, fears, conditioning and simply learning to live in a state of perpetual inertia. At the same time, our body too has a rhythm during which we perform at our best. The energy ebbs during the day. Thus, we have a very small window within which we can do something really path-breaking.

So where does our time go in general? Let's look at the usual elements in our day and how much time they on an average consume.

Daily Time Analysis

	Major Categories	Time (Hours)
1	Sleeping	7 - 9
2	Getting Ready	1 - 1.5
3	Commuting	1 - 2
4	Working	8 - 9
5	Eating (All Meals)	1 - 1.5
	Remaining Hours	Depends upon Above
	Total Hours	24

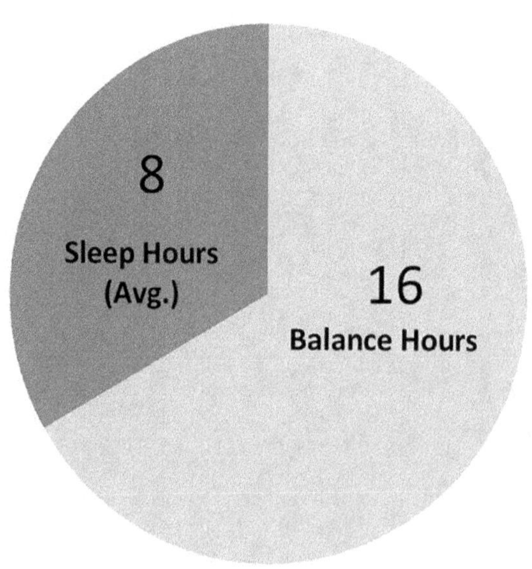

Sleep is one of the pivotal factors around which Master of the Day philosophy is based. The vigour for the day comes from the sleep quality and quantity both. Thus, it is very critical that sleep is not compromised under any circumstances. An afternoon nap is also a great re-energizer if your schedule and circumstances can permit. It is estimated that you need as little as 20 minutes of sleep to get refreshed, regain the energy and concentration that had started ebbing. Sleeping for longer than 30 minutes puts you under the deep sleep cycle after which if you have to wake-up you will be feeling groggy and inactive. Thus, it is very important that the time of 20-30 minutes is never crossed. Keep an alarm to ensure that you don't get into a deep sleep.

We spend about a third of our lives sleeping. The Washington based National Sleep Foundation (NSF) conducted a global study led by a multidisciplinary expert panel which recommended Younger adults (18-25):7-9 hours, Adults (26-64):7 to 9 hours and Older adults (65+):7-8 hours. The sleep requirements are even more for teenagers, younger children, and infants.

Leaving aside our "Sleeping Hours" we are left with 15-17 hours which basically is our "Up-time". What we do with these 15-17 hours determines what we achieve in a day. However, if we cut down on our sleep hours, we run the risk of being less than effective during the day. The extra hour or two that you snatch from your sleep hours will show up in being late by approximately the same time the next morning , missing on the "Golden Hours" and being less alert during the day. Those few hours of your night time has the potential to derail a big chunk of "Up-time" that you have the next day.

In a nutshell, we spend our "Up-time" on activities like grooming and preparing for work/business, commuting, working (the biggest chunk), eating and the balance time gets spent with self (sitting idle, checking phone, watching TV, exercising etc.), family and socially.

Now coming to the working hours, it is estimated that even when we are deep into work, we are likely to waste a lot of time doing work that does not add much value and doing things in a sub-optimal way. The fact is that time is spent in small crevices of the day measured in seconds, minutes, hours and it slips away slowly and surreptitiously. Time, thus, is either a part of our life or we can live our lives oblivious of it.

If we can work with a focus on our priorities; work efficiently, lead a healthy life, are earning per our expectations then probably we don't need to become more educated on time management. This is however not the case. In reality, our today is already in custody of our tomorrow or is roaming in the past. We are either perpetually in a state of going to do but not getting anything significant done or are searching for answers from the knowledge garnered in the past and trying the same old tired scripts that have clearly not succeeded in bringing you the success that you deserve.

At the same time by putting off today's work for the future we are tripping many of the tasks that will become urgent tomorrow. Tomorrow becomes even busier and leaves you even more frustrated. Time doesn't lapse and neither can we manage it. Thus, for measuring and controlling our day we need a structure and a set of objectives which can serve as the criteria for success.

Exercise: *From this moment onwards grab a small notebook and start recording how you are spending your time. Also track how you are feeling like energetic, listless, tired etc. Keep doing this daily and patterns will start emerging. Record the time for events like Waking up, Bed Time, Starting for Work, Getting up from Work and all the meals that you have taken. The exercise will seem like a drag but it will help compile data analysis of which can change the course of your life. After a couple of weeks, you will have amazing data to analyze.*

2.4 THE MONEY AND TIME CORRELATION

Our day is filled up with activities that we call work. Man is a machine and that machine has to do work at the very least for its survival. In the civilized world, the provisions for leading a good life are by having money. The reason people work is to earn money which in turn can be used to take care of their basic needs be it hunger, shelter, security and right up to their status and comfort. For making money many of us work for others or have our businesses. The need for money rises in proportion to where we are located. For example, as we move away from a city to say, a remote village, time seems to slow down simply because the cues to spending money are missing and we don't feel the need to splurge. The distractions to our senses which are heightened by corporate marketing strategies are minimal or their access is restricted so the need or propensity to spend money is significantly lower. We quickly climb down the needs hierarchy to fulfilling our basic needs and suddenly the basal state of our existence i.e. happiness appears. The deeper we live within clusters of human civilization like big cities, the more we need money to manage our life. Here, all signs of freedom and things that are free in nature like fruits, vegetables, clean air, water, are removed from our sight and a price tag is attached to them. In a big city, everything from basic needs to status needs costs more and their consumption is significantly higher. Needs are continuously being stoked by quick gratification which can only be done through money and that means through work. Thus, the need for money is more acutely felt depending upon our needs. Money demands time and appears to make it run faster.

At the same time rising inflation and consumerism go hand in hand in decreasing the purchasing power of money while the needs increase. Just to highlight how the present era like no time else has heightened the need to have money, let's look at the contrasting period way back in the eighties which I remember vividly.

We were part of the burgeoning Indian middle class in the eighties, yet to be liberated on thoughts of materialism and paying for an object of desire not a bit more than its intended utility value. My parents aspired to buy the essential home luxuries like a color television, some decent furniture, a video recorder, and a small car. That's it! That was how high they desired to sprawl their legs in the lap of luxury. They aspired but never ever crossed the limit where spending money could be considered tantamount to splurging.

As a kid, I had all the time in the world. Why was it so? It was simply because I didn't have to worry about earning money. Later when earning money became a necessity, I had to lend my time to someone to earn it.

Slowly, money becomes the all-important determinant leading to contentment and happiness. We progressively forget that things that gave us joy as a child didn't have any monetary value . Those hours spent playing or chatting with friends, taking a walk in the park, spending time with parents, siblings, wife, kids and small activities don't have a price tag attached.

Compare it to the present time when well- known brands kneel and kiss to win more converts and online shopping makes owning material objects ridiculously easy. Come to think of it, the humble government built two-bedroom dwelling that my father bought in the eighties was lesser than the price of the latest iphone! Salaries were meagre then but one that would meet basic needs and leave space for talk, play and lead a contented life.

I remember the joy of getting my first iPhone not just because of the premium tech but that it was presented to me by someone special. I cherish the "sentimental value" not the "object value" which in any case soon became outdated. So intuitively, a part of our mind knows what gives us joy but we are so stuck up with the objects of desire (and which obviously cost money) that we brush aside all the thoughts of joy that is within our reach, for another day. In the end, people may die rich but their time runs out!

Materialism demands attention and tends to take centre stage of our existence once we fall for its charms. Owning a phone today is not sufficient. One must adorn and magnify it with flashy covers, protective screens, chargers, headphones, speakers and much more . Minimalism on the other hand leaves you to lead your life oblivious of what others expect you to be. Materialism creates its own virtual world of needs offset from what our soul desires. While we chase our hedonistic material dreams life passes us by quietly in the form of a kid's laughter, a blooming garden, a walk in the silent woods, a light chat with our parents and in a million other ways we no longer recognize. Life happens and flows quietly all around us. Once in a while we wake from our existential slumber till we reach for our phone again!

Work is essential to earn money for our basic survival to providing the luxury stuff which are more driven by status and self-actualization needs. But, work involves more than the use of tools and techniques. Whatever may be the nature of work, the fact remains that money is given only when a person commits to spending time at someone's premises doing specified work. Thus, a complete chunk of time has to be dedicated.

Thus, time will always be at a premium if you are working or have your own business. Tense work environment and time pressure lead people to spend their off-work hours relaxing through various means; personal gadgets, external entertainment spots like restaurants, shopping malls, cinemas, amusement parks etc. which again places demands on your time & money.

We all would have heard the concept of "time is money" but we never put 'time' on the same pedestal as 'money'. No way! We have no qualms in spending it mercilessly and without a clue on where our time is spent. Thus, procrastinators at least cannot be called misers. As far as time is concerned we spend it lavishly on anything that catches our fancy.

So ingrained is the concept of money as the ultimate pursuit in us that we dedicate our lives to garner more and more of it. Ask an old but rich person on something they wish their money could buy and most likely you would hear the word that, if possible, they would like to turn back the clock or would like to have more time. But, money and time are not interchangeable. Money can be earned back but the time spent is irreversible!

In the next chapter, we will analyze some of the key factors which are responsible for our day to turn into a damp squib. These are factors which are present all around us and in our work methods. But, till the time, these are understood we cannot act upon them in a structured way. Once we understand their role, the improvement efforts can then begin in real earnest. Let's look at them.

What keeps us away from success?

The time is out of joint...O cursed spite.
That ever I was born to set it right.
William Shakespeare

Let us analyze the reason why our day fluctuates between fixed schedules to blatant time waste. Our habits and behaviors further ensure that we continue to lose the most precious periods of a typical day. We will analyze the key factors which spoil the day for us or prevent us from utilizing our day effectively. There are essentially three categories of factors which spoil our day. These three categories are what we will term as "Starting Potential", "Wastes in a Day", and " Effectiveness Destroyers". The Starting Potential makes it difficult and sometimes almost impossible to start work. The "Wastes in a Day" ensure that whatever we may do will take a huge amount of time and effort. Understand, that the real work or actions that take us forward in life consumes very little time. A decision to act, or perform an action can take ridiculously less amount of time, sometimes just minutes but we may take forever to reach that moment! The "Effectiveness Destroyers" are a cluster of factors that kills productivity and gets us sub-optimal results.

3.1 THE STARTING POTENTIAL

Before we move on to the other concepts we must understand one of the key factors which determine what gets done and what remains pending. This is, in fact, a combination of a number of other factors. We will coin a term over here called the *Starting Potential*. It is the resistance we have to start doing any work and then completing it. The reasons may be physical or mental. In common parlance, we may call it procrastination but the concept of starting potential goes a step further and actually unravels the mystery surrounding our disinclination to start work.

Starting Potential is the minimum energy that you need to expend before getting started. It is the resistance we have to doing the work and then completing it. A simple rule to understand is that if the thing that you have to do is all set-up and you have all the things you need to do before you, the chances of getting it done increase dramatically.

Even electricity needs a potential difference to flow. Otherwise, it's just a mass of electrons sitting in one corner vibrating and colliding with one another without any direction. Similarly, we also need to identify a potential difference between where we are and where we can be if we take that pending action. In our case, either it has to be induced through external pressure or we have to have that passion for achieving the desired end state. We are driven by our passion or need if and only if the job at hand has a big impact, negative or positive. Anything else and we get into a stupor or simply push the job down our priority list. Many times this is because we don't evaluate the benefits or consequences of not taking the action. Even if we want to take action, disorganization comes in the way. It could also be just hesitation because we are not clear about the steps to be taken. Thus, starting potential can stem from unawareness about the consequences, lack of clarity or even disorganization.

At the same time, any job we begin executing and then leave incomplete also starts developing the starting potential. As soon as we stop doing a task, the starting potential starts rising again. It is most of the time directly proportional to the duration that lapses when it is again picked up. Slowly, either we lose track, forget who we spoke to or what all we did and where did we keep the stuff we prepared etc. Thus it is very important to finish work at one go or keep the threads alive by keeping on working on them to minimize it. Never leave a job incomplete. It sends the message that it doesn't matter or carrying an incomplete job is fine

3.1.1 SOME IMPORTANT CONCEPTS

The concepts described here will play a crucial part in analyzing why we underachieve during our day and are unable to do work optimally. They are also linked to lowering the starting potential being described here.

SET-UP TIME

"Set-up time" is the time required to start a new task or resume the task from where we left. Countless distractions happen throughout our day. Each distraction takes us out of our 'flow' and our brain has to warm up again. Ideally, we would like to put quality time into key tasks. But our days are made of small chunks of time, and each time we switch tasks or get distracted we lose a small chunk.

The starting potential is our constant enemy, every time we come back to finish a job. We need time to again recollect, organize, concentrate and execute on the same piece of work. Set-up time may include things like arranging the documents required, sifting through related e-mails, organizing stationery, talking to someone to get clarity or any other preparation that may be required.

CHANGEOVER TIME

Another concept closely related with Set-up time is that of the Changeover Time. It is the time taken to switch between two core tasks or make the transition from one phase of the day to the other. Both of these scenarios are similar as going to office is a changeover and we need set-up time in the form of grooming, preparing and commuting for office before we can begin work. To switch between tasks you will need to have all the stuff, information, support and clarity that you need to begin the next task immediately after finishing the current one.

THREADS

We don't start big projects and procrastinate because they seem daunting. They appear like a mountain which we have to overcome. This is the reason we don't even start.It's like "Eating an Elephant" which is a metaphor for a big, scary and hairy project which can be made to look much more feasible and plausible if we break it down into smaller parts. In this book, we will refer to these small parts as "Threads". Threads make "Eat the Elephant" approach possible. It's like slicing a big project so it can be consumed gradually depending upon the time available. Threads are steps in a project which may or may not have a dependency on each other but collectively are required to accomplish the project. Thus it is very important to finish work at one go or keep the threads alive by keeping on working them one by one. Ideally, you should have one task or thread which should be active and once that is over, you should pick up the next. Threads have to be specific and must be progressive i.e. they must lead us to the next thread. Understand the magnitude, the difficulty involved and the support required and execute accordingly. Threads are the real value adds which takes our project closer to our dream. If they seem to be consuming a lot of time or are too complex, consider slicing them further.

3.1.2 STRATEGIES

There are some strategies that you can apply to overcome the starting potential. Here are a few of the important ones that should become a part and parcel of your routine.

Get Organized: "Out of sight, out of mind" is a golden maxim that triggers the starting potential. It further aggravates as our memory of what we had done earlier becomes paler day by day. On top of that, all that we need to accomplish that task; the strip of paper where you noted down that piece of information, the conversation that you had with someone, the form you started filling up but left midway and many more such acts pile up and starts creating a layer of inactivity around the task which you will find hard to shake-off the next time you revisit the task again after a gap. The Starting Potential is this "layer". Organization reduces "starting potential" significantly. Keep all the stuff related to a particular task at one place or file, mention notes, and important dates, keep a log, have a time-bound plan, place reminders and your task will get done much sooner.

Just Get Started: Perhaps the best way to break the starting potential is to simply start without preparation or a plan. There is an indescribable grace about getting started; Soon all the things that you forgot and your strength comes right back and you are connected. The starting potential will start evaporating as you start galloping forward.

Understand the Reason: Just ask yourself the question as to why you are not starting the work? The actual reasons if you dig a bit deeper may be very surprising. Some usual reasons you may come up with may be like the ones given below

- "I feel that I will not be able to sustain this later"
- "I am too busy"
- "I have not yet made up my mind"
- "I don't have the money"
- "I feel bored"
- "I don't think this will work"
- "It will take a long time and I have ten other things to do"
- "I am not clear what needs to be done "

But if you want to unravel the root cause then there is a beautiful technique called the "5 Why Analysis" which helps to reach the root cause of the issues, unproductive behaviors and any problem for which a solution doesn't seem apparent. It is said that only by asking "why" 5 times, successfully can you delve into a problem deeply enough to understand the actual root cause. By the time you get to the 4th and 5th "Why" you are likely to approach the root cause of the problem.

To explain this technique, there is a very interesting example quoted by Benjamin Franklin in Poor Richard's Almanac in 1758. The point he was essentially trying to make was that "A little neglect may breed great mischief,". It went something like this

For want of a nail a shoe was lost,

For want of a shoe a horse was lost,

For want of a horse a rider was lost,

For want of a rider an army was lost,

For want of an army a battle was lost,

For want of a battle the war was lost,

For want of the war the kingdom was lost,

And all for the want of the little horseshoe nail!

While the exact origins and interpretation of these lines is difficult to ascertain but in essence it comes down to the realization that seemingly trivial reasons or hidden reasons are responsible for big and sometimes catastrophic outcomes.

Here is a small illustration of 5 Why analysis in real life

I am late for Work

Why?

There was too much traffic

Why?

I got up late

Why?

I slept very late

Why?

I went to a party and had drinks one too many

Why?

I normally am late and am not able to say no to friends requests to stay back.

There you are, by the 5th "Why" you have got the root reason and other reasons why you were late. It seems that you stay back at parties to please the hosts and are unable to say "No" to extra drinks. So, getting up late after a late night party is because of the lack of assertiveness in leaving early.

You can use this technique as frequently as you want to understand the real root cause reasons.

Whatever may be the reason, re-think the perspective. Identifying the core reason is only one of the methods which will enable you to attack the starting potential. Look at the repercussions of not doing the task or the benefits that finishing the task brings. If the work that you are dithering over has to be done sooner or later then why not plan it right now?

3.2 THE WASTES IN A DAY

Despite your best intentions, a day is prone to be hijacked by a number of wastes which are present in our day to day activities. The wastes in the day make us less productive, prone to delays and ultimately lead to non-performance in areas which matter the most. The way we perform work is a process and these value destroyers can afflict all or some of the steps of this process. Very simply, if we are not taking action, we are not getting anywhere. Action is the only real value addition and only this matters. Here we must differentiate between value enablers and pure waste. Value enablers are activities that help to plan for action and execute it. Included in value enablers are activities like planning, scheduling, researching, checking, approving etc. These activities help prepare for action and ensure quality and speed. Thus value enablers are not wastes. But having too many value enablers in a task will again be a waste.

The factors listed below can be considered to be pure wastes and don't add any value to your efforts. They end up prolonging the completion of work, increase effort and can even stall work. They are also one of the key reasons behind procrastination.

▶ **Carrying a Work Inventory**: We carry in our head or otherwise, a long list of unprocessed work that needs to be done, unsolved puzzles, things that are not clear to us, work that worries us, delays, and guilt pangs for not devoting time to important areas of our life like family, health, relaxation etc. The list seems endless and we are unable to cope with the deluge of work. There is work that we still have to start, while we have not even decided on a few tasks while some others may be in progress. However, the fact is that work not completed doesn't add any value to our life. Carrying excess inventory will bog you down. Ideally, you should have one task or thread which should be active and once that is over, you should pick up the next. That decision to invest your money which can secure your future never gets started because we have either not decided, or not contacted a financial consultant or not given the final signed papers of submission etc. The end result is zero!

Similarly carrying clutter leads to disorganization & waste of money. Just look at the cupboards/racks and other storage spaces within your home and workplace. You may be carrying stuff like clothes, papers, books, stationery, gadgets which you no longer use. They add to the "Visual noise" around you and is sometimes referred to as *clutter*.

Slowly, we get resigned to the fact that all this talk about balance in life or being able to plan our day is well-nigh impossible to achieve. *The work can pile-up at various stages of our work process. At the same time, we also have to see that not all incoming work needs to be processed.* There is no point in carrying inventory if we do not plan to work on it.

▶ **Waiting Unnecessarily**: Waiting is perhaps the biggest waste that we excel in. Anytime we are waiting for something we are not adding value! Right here right now, you can get up and start changing your life and within no time get into a different zone, but various factors are at play which ensures that we keep waiting as if in a stupor. We wait endlessly for taking action or making decisions that might stretch on till eternity. We might get that warm feeling that it is on our "To Do" list but we never get around to doing it. It might be a skin rash that irritates us but the doctor seems to be on another planet and we procrastinate endlessly, or it could be the life-sucking job which we religiously get up and go to and come back even more jaded. Understand that this is your "comfort zone" exercising a gravity pull to keep you where you are. Anytime we are not taking action we are technically waiting. It all boils down to action. Action takes you forward and creates value and growth for you. Being wrong is fine; remaining inactive is "death". Sometimes, thinking can be a waste of time. We may convince ourselves that we will take action after thinking over it but we still don't do it.

▶ **Gold Plating your Work**: Gold plating is a metaphorical term for overdoing a task or a project step. We tend to brood endlessly on decisions, never ending actions, or simply get stuck in a per-fectionist mindset wherein actual gold may elude us but "gold plating" is what we achieve. And, that gold comes from our own time, effort and mental peace. So we gold plate the report we send, spend endless time to look at the same thing over and over again or take an eternity to make "perfect" decisions. Gold plating is a waste if it doesn't add any value to what you are doing.

▶ **Over-Production**: This waste simply put is to produce more than what is required. Carrying too many tasks in your mind, trying to multi-task and taking on too much on yourself is a sure sign that you are overproducing. You cannot sustain it, nor can you ever meet your goals. What matters is quality, not the quantity.

In one of the organizations that I worked for, PowerPoint was next to God. Virtually anything that was documented was on PowerPoint and it had to be perfected so much so that there was an official reference manual that prescribed what format to use for a particular type of a presentation for e.g. budget, strategy, quality etc. We had a monthly meeting with our Managing Director. Our MD was a stickler for details. All of a sudden he would ask us about an issue or how a past data trend compares with the present one. If someone failed to answer he would publicly humiliate that person. Thus, our manager would involve himself and virtually the entire team in preparing for that meeting one week in advance. We would leave aside all our work and started preparing extra slides of comparisons with trends, data analysis, creating beautiful slides that were repeatedly and excessively formatted. We used to spend many days preparing for this one-hour presentation. Clearly, we were over-producing and over-processing to preclude any embarrassment. Collectively we were wasting the time of the entire team on an activity which though very important was not just gold plating but also overproduction.

▶ **Rework**: Rework as the name suggest is about working again on the same piece of work. It multiplies our work without adding any value. It's like visiting a task multiple times to understand it better, make corrections or just for improving upon it. The problem with this approach is that we lose the momentum and again create the starting potential when restarting the work. After a while, with this kind of an approach, we start getting diminishing returns as the work has not seen completion, it's not shipped and is adding to our incomplete work inventory. Try to complete the task at one-go or thread it to keep chipping at it keeping a deadline in sight. In our daily life, this waste manifests in the form of wrong reports, wrong analysis, wrong shipments, material or product rejections and even incomplete or wrongly understood communications.

▶ **Unnecessary Motion / Transportation**: The more disorganized we are, the more we tend to move around. We spend time getting up from our workplace numerous times for fetching one thing or the other. Similarly, commuting is another example where a lot of time is wasted waiting in traffic or for covering long distances. We want to visit an exotic location lying thousands of miles away just to register that we were there. A similar experience maybe available at a nearby location saving time and money both. Going on holidays to far-flung places may have merit but, at the end of the day, if we are more stressed and tired than relaxed, the entire purpose of having a rejuvenating holiday is defeated.

The wasted motions are not just physical but also mental. Every time we multi-task our mind jumps from one activity to another and in the end, we are stressed out without getting much achieved. An organized workplace, computer, and your thinking habits can ensure that all unnecessary energy-sapping motion can be minimized or even eliminated.

▶ **Waste of Intellect**: Keeping at a job that under-utilizes you is a classic case of a waste of intellect. People day in and day out keep doing the same thing which is well below their true potential and the gap between what they could be and what they are sometimes can kill people mentally and physically. The verve is gone and soon manifests in their indulging in excesses like overeating, drinking, smoking. The spiral of self-deprecation continues and few are again able to come out it. Apart from this working at sub-par productivity, missing golden hours to start some creative threads also falls under the underutilization of intellect category.

The wastes mentioned above can lead to incredible time waste or can disorient you totally and keeps you from closing even simple tasks. Don't habituate them, remain cognizant of their presence throughout your day and you will soon begin to reduce their magnitude and ultimately eliminate them from your life.

3.3 NOISE

The noise is one single factor that keeps you away from focussing. It is not the ambient sound waves going above comfortable decibel levels but the incessant noise in your head and around you which makes you go swinging wildly in all directions or if suppressed won't let you focus on things that really count.

Noise simply put are tasks and thoughts which prevents you from focussing on your highest priorities till the time it's eliminated. A cluster of such unattended tasks and delays can increase the intensity of noise. The noise could be anything from not starting to work on an important task for the day, small pending nagging tasks like making payments, follow-ups, distractions that litter your day, things that distract you, makes you lazy or any lack of a plan or direction that prevents you from working focussedly and persistently on a key task.

For example, you have to send someone information to continue the work. It could be your tax or insurance consultant or one of your colleagues. If you do not send it, soon the processing will stop so it's up to you how soon you send it to keep things in motion. This is still a situation where there is still pressure on you to act. What happens if it is just left to you to do a task when there is no pressure? You have the option of doing it now or later. It may soon slip out of your mind. For example, one of the best daily habits that can materially change your life is your habit to maintain your daily expenses. But, if we don't habituate this, the task would almost surely will get side-lined or you may pick it at the end of the week when you have to again look for and remind yourself of the expenses you have made.

There is a huge starting potential to be taken care of. Same is the case with other self-management tasks like cleaning up your wardrobe or fixing an appointment with your doctor to show the skin rash you have been scratching all week, visiting an ailing relative or it could be as small as getting the broken strap of your watch repaired. They remain in your memory troubling you but never getting done. You put up with the pain of finding clothes in a messy wardrobe or wearing your back-up watch instead of your favorite one because you never get around to getting that new battery replaced for it. These are some of the various facets of noise we encounter in our day to day life.

The construct below shows how our basal state is covered by layers upon layers of non-homogenous thoughts and thinking patterns that play havoc with our ability to focus on the present. Noise needs to be managed as one of the outermost layers which interfaces with the conscious world and is affected by other deeper layers of thoughts and their impact on us. It needs to be managed proactively as it directly can lift our productivity several notches if we have to focus and become significantly faster and effective than we are at present.

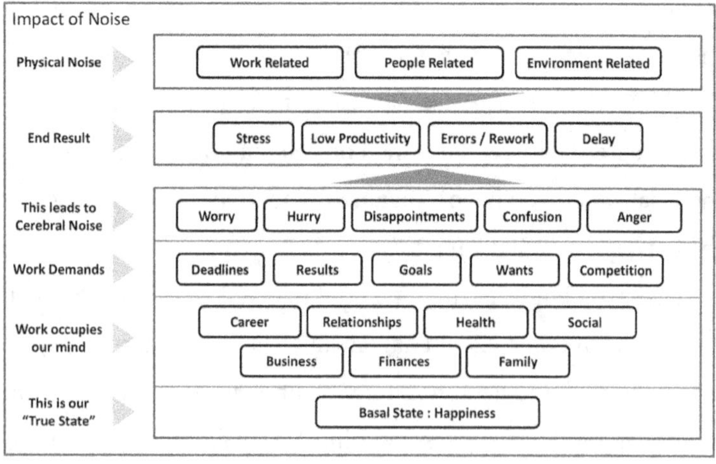

For achieving your goals you must manage the noise around you so you can focus on what's important. Given below are the different types of possible noise. It is by no means a complete list. You may like to add your own list of distractions. However, the approach required to contain it remains the same.

CEREBRAL NOISE

This type of noise can also be in the form of worry, anger, anxiety, confusion which keeps our mind fuzzy, disoriented and maybe even overwhelmed by it. Apart from this, a lack of clarity, indecision or disorganization can also trigger cerebral noise. Thus, it is imperative that you start your day with issues sorted out and minimize the noise in your head. Following the "Master of the Day" plan will ensure that noise is surgically isolated, clustered and disposed of at non-peak hours.

You must develop strategies and new ways of thinking and tackling the problems that plague you. Remember all the problems that are around us are just events that are around us have to be managed. There is always an elegant solution to every problem. The problem arises when we try to ignore the issue or don't develop effective strategies to deal with it. Don't wait for your problems to multiply or grow, tackle them right away and move on.

TASK OR ACTIVITY RELATED

Task or Activity related noise can be tasks of small duration which have to be tackled or else they can turn urgent and trip important tasks during the day and during the week. These can come in various shapes like pending payments, household chores, making a follow-up call or also can be in the form of some external disruption. However, many of these tasks are of very short duration which can be eliminated in short bursts of activity.

PEOPLE RELATED

People can distract you in multiple ways. They can call, drop-in, send e-mails, invite you for meetings, request favours and send chat / text messages. They may have a genuine reason and you may even decide to lend an ear or even actually help. It's your call but when the disturbance is avoidable and inconsiderate then one of the biggest time savers you can employ here is to learn the art of saying "No". You may develop various ways in which you can politely or assertively say a "No" depending upon urgency, your own task at hand, your ability to help and many other factors that might govern your choice. It will save you a lot of time and frustration. The proactive mode is the best way to manage small tasks.

ENVIRONMENT RELATED

This type of noise can come from your immediate environment. It could be the ambient noise around you. It could be a phone that suddenly shrieks for attention, people chatting incessantly in close vicinity, asking for a favour or your manager calling you at his seat and then keeping you waiting. Don't let it get off your core tasks. If ambient noise is an issue, ear buds or earphones are an effective solution. Play some light calming music and your productivity may also go a few notches higher. Another effective strategy is that of isolation. Move to a location where you can concentrate more.

THE EFFECT OF THESE DISTRACTIONS

Distractions are our mind wandering off even before we start serious work or in the middle of it. We don't realize the impact of it till when we return to it and find that it's so difficult to get back into the zone. Pure unadulterated time is, thus, a must if you really want to achieve something. When we drop an important task for a less important one, we give up our focus, our success which will get delayed or may even get short-circuited indefinitely. Once we are off an important and urgent task the starting potential starts rising and it will again take "Set-up time" to resume the task from where you left. Countless distractions happen throughout your day. Each of them takes you out of your 'flow' and then your brain has to warm up again. Ideally, you would like to have to put quality time into key tasks. But our days are made of small pieces, and each time we switch tasks or get distracted we lose a small piece. Slowly these pieces add up until we wonder where the day went. Do everything in your power to keep your day intact. Because once your day gets cut into tiny pieces, you're not in control anymore.

But what happens after the distraction is over is even worse. When you go from one task to another, you don't instantly start performing that new task efficiently. Your brain needs time to become familiar with the new task. To make your schedule more accurate, we need to add the amount of time it takes you to switch tasks.

THE SELF-INFLICTED DISTRACTION – MULTI-TASKING

Multi-tasking looks great but in effect it leads to sub-optimal productivity. You create a series of incompletes that will add to your noise. If we are multi-tasking, we are very much engaged but flipping back and forth from one task to another leaves our mind slower and much more prone to distraction. The MOD routine may look like multi-tasking at first glance but there is a big difference, it requires us to focus on one task at a time and then make a quick changeover to the next category, task or project. Switching between work is one of the key skills, that you will be learning as part of this routine.

MANAGING NOISE

Ideally, you should have zero noise during the execution of your priority tasks. The MOD routine that you will design soon is dependent upon how you tackle noise henceforth. Much of this noise can be killed then and there until and unless you let the decibel levels to go out of control in which case you will have to dedicate slots to tackle several noise items all at once. Noise has to be subdued and controlled. Getting early in the morning is one key step towards driving noise out of your day. You will have to muster the will to tackle noise as it requires some starting potential to be overcome.

Here is a general methodology for managing noise.

METHODOLOGY

1. **Calm Yourself**: Cerebral Noise might be the most difficult noise to control. Concentrate your mind by following a daily calming ritual like meditation, yoga or pick from various mindfulness techniques which have become very popular these days. Also, as a step towards attaining public leadership, decide that you will attain personal leadership by resolving that nothing can ruffle your sense of calm through the day. This is one of the critical life skill that you can learn, that will hold you in good stead whatever you may be up against.

2. **Plan to Focus**: Preparing the Master of the Day plan will cut-out much of the noise and confine most of it into one cluster in which it can be executed. Give some time for your mind to focus. When you are in the zone, the noise will recede into the background. Don't try to multi-task. If you are working on a priority task, then be assured that it will get you results provided you take it to completion.

3.4 THE EFFECTIVENESS DESTROYERS

The effectiveness of what we do is not only dependent upon our resistance to start work or the noise but also on a host of factors which play an important part in the way we select, understand process and complete work. Together with Starting Potential and Noise these factors which we can call as "Effectiveness Destroyers" forms a trio of "Value Killers" which dampens the inclination to start and depletes subsequent productivity. We will look at these factors again in the coming chapters from a management perspective.

1 The never ending list of things we have to do

Our day begins with a collection of work that needs our attention and action. Whether we pay attention to it on that same day, next week or next month depends upon the choice we make and how we track and execute it. We might think that we will act upon it sooner or later, the need is there, the intention is there but accompanying action doesn't follow. These activities keep coming and going out of our mind as and when we are reminded of them. This gives rises to a sense of continuous dissatisfaction that we are not taking action or focusing on important areas of our lives but soon we get occupied in something else and forget about it. These thoughts are like trains passing you by as you stand at a station. You are just a frequent observer to these "train of thoughts". Our mind is a poor retainer of "immediate information". It will definitely register that some action has to be taken but it will not place it in a pecking order to execute till the time we consciously evolve mechanisms to create a list of actions and an execution plan. We have to thus find a way through which we can ensure that we no longer have to keep everything in our head and can rely on a system to catch incoming work and execute or store to deal with it later.

2 Never sure what to choose

From the time we get up from bed to the time we retire to the same bed, we are making tens of choices. From deciding upon the time to wake up, brush, bathe, clothes that we wear, time to leave for office and other professional and personal choices, we make them throughout the day even without being conscious about it. Every moment we are making choices that determine the course of our day, week months, years and then our entire life. We as human beings can consciously make choices right from managing the mundane basic necessities of life to making decisions on achieving our true potential.

While we do make choices but we may ignore or sidetrack burning issues which can make a qualitative difference to our life. These choices may not seem so urgent at one level but are nevertheless very important as they can be life-changing events. The urgent choices impose themselves on you and may seem inordinately important because of the immediate repercussions that you may have to face. For example, if there is a looming deadline to pay your taxes then obviously you will leave aside other tasks and focus on it as late submission may involve penalties and failure to take into account all aspects of it may lead to monetary losses.

Compare this to making an investment that will secure your future or can give you great returns. This is something that is totally in your hands but there is no deadline to meet. It is for you to grab hold of it and get it done and enhance your life. You have to create that urgency! Similarly, a task like looking for jobs online and sending your resume is important if you are stuck in a boring and life-sapping job but it does not seem that way! We are the master of our body and mind. Every moment we are making a decision about what we are doing consciously or subconsciously. What we eat, drink and do is being determined by us. We are creatures of habits, beliefs, mental makeup and act accordingly so much so that if you follow your daily tracks, you will be amazed at the regularity of your actions, thought patterns and beliefs.

Making a choice is easier said than done. Your rational mind may say something but we end up doing exactly the opposite? Why? People drink and smoke and even take drugs even though all of them are proven to be addictive and outright bad for our health. Why people continue to stick to jobs or relationships which suck the life out of them. They grumble all along the way but never seem to come around to taking the choice to freedom.

Sometimes dropping a task or a target is also a choice. If during decision making it turns out that you have to make some tough choices then we may procrastinate if it's not urgent. Immediately we return to a state of low energy as before. Our body doesn't seem to mind it. Slowly, not taking decisions, especially difficult ones becomes a habit. We prefer to remain mediocre, remain stuck in the same job, or keep incurring losses in a high demand low yield business. We do everything except making a choice coming out of a decision.

The fact is that this very moment you can choose to take a decision or an action in one of the most critical areas of your life and get ahead in life. This very moment! But, will you take it?

3 Getting that hidden "Go Ahead' in our mind

You may have put tasks on your work list but still don't do it. Why? It doesn't figure in your priorities and doesn't really make an impact. But if you stop for a moment and delve on the repercussions of not doing the task or the reward of doing it, maybe you will get the reason that you were lacking earlier. That is the time you have taken a "Go / No Go" decision. Unfortunately, there are many other such decisions which remain in our head. Sometimes forever!

Our mind as mentioned earlier is a poor retainer of information.

It's like a RAM of a computer. Whatever is there at a moment might soon get erased or eclipsed by whatever next task is loaded into it. But unlike a RAM, the task remains somewhere in our mind and depending upon the importance it might just stick around. However, carrying the load of a task which we can forget is a stress by itself. Thus, our effort should be to evolve a process to capture the task at the earliest on some permanent medium which can be referenced later. This done, you can focus on the tasks at hand and come back to these parked tasks later.

This is the first step towards reaching anywhere. But before we move further it is worthwhile to clarify what is a decision. A decision or an intention to act is an alignment of your core values, inclinations, talent and your agreement on taking the actions necessary to achieve your goal. The reason that we don't achieve what we aspire to achieve is not because of the fact that we lack the ability. It is because we never really decided to go for it. We never reached a point when we said enough is enough. There is a very simple relation that explains why not all thoughts translate into action. In an ideal scenario, this should be a correlation between our thoughts and subsequent actions i.e. the thoughts should result in action.

Thoughts = Action

However, that is not the case, especially for thoughts that force us to come out of our comfort zone. The Missing factor is the decision that we have to make to convert thoughts into action. An intention is generated after we have made a decision to act upon it. The complete relation now becomes as follows,

Thought or Idea + Decision = Intention to Act

In fact, this is the first natural pull that you can apply to get started. Unfortunately, the majority of people aspire for a lot of things but have decided on none of them. Thus their dreams remain unfulfilled. A decision or an intention to act is the most important part of reaching your goal. Rest is just your figuring out how to reach your goal, whose help is required, how you arrange for it and being ready to face the consequences (if any) of your action. The beauty of your decision is that action seems to be the natural culmination of it.

The Bhagwad Geeta, one of the revered religious text of the Hindus, is a set of conversations that happen between Pandav prince Arjuna who is out in the battlefield facing a battle of dynastic supremacy. Arjuna, despite being a brave and peerless shooter is troubled by thoughts of what the outcome of the war will be and the deaths that will occur on both sides of people who are his own kin.

Lord Krishna understanding his predicament gave forth the concept of Karma Yoga. It provides us the spiritual perspective of discharging our work within the confines of a day. In chapter three of the Geeta, Krishna reasons that Karmayoga in the most simplest form ordains one to discharge their duties whatever they maybe without thinking about the material comfort it will bring. Whether the results of the action are pleasant or unpleasant, they bind one to the bondage of repeated birth and death in the material world. Therefore, one should work in a way that will not further entangle one in material bondage but will lead to ultimate liberation. An exclusive attachment to fruits and immediate gratification consequences can prevent us from discharging our dharma (ethical action).

Big decisions are never easy. They come with a huge emotional component which may have to bear because of the decision, Remember, we are not going to be here permanently and we may not get the chance to make the same decision later. So it's fine to make mistakes, if this is what your heart desires, and you know it will make you happy, go ahead and take the plunge.

4 The lack of clarity in what we do

Clarity is about what needs to be done and how. But even before that, the purpose of why we have to take a particular action should become clear. Once we are clear about the purpose, the intention to act becomes even stronger. Add passion to it and the person becomes an unstoppable force. Confusion disappears and one can see what it will take to get it done. This is the beginning of fluidity. Your mind loves clarity and coupled with focus it turns into a lethal combination.

The tendency to see work as composed of a one single mass emanates because either we don't know what are the steps to be taken or may not have given a thought to it. But one thing is clear, for every work there is a way to get it done elegantly and on-time. The more you build the starting potential and delay the work, the worse it will become. One day when you may get around to doing it, you may realize how easy it was in the first place.

Sometimes the task is very simple but in our minds, we don't see the priority and the fact that it is so easy to achieve. Hence, even before even attempting we give up. Getting clarity is one of the most important things to get started. You immediately increase the probability of doing a job that becomes clear to you. One of the best ways I have found to do something daunting is to speak to people who have done it before. You will realize that initially, they have had the same fears and apprehensions but they still went ahead and made it. Even in the absence of clarity you can visualize the task and see it within your mind. Many of the things that are required are the ones which you may have done before and intuitively fathom what a particular task will involve based upon your logic and experience. This itself will take you towards clarity and this ability is available in abundance in you.

5 The disorder around us

Getting organized is about taking a huge step forward towards reclaiming our life. Getting organized is about clarity and not having to spend time looking for things. Getting organized is not having to spend time setting up your work.

If you want to be a super performer, the "Master of the Day" and much more, then you have to be immaculately organized. That's a small price to pay for being happier, healthier, richer and better, all in a day.

A human being has a limited field of vision. Anything within sight of vision is always going to catch our attention. The proverb "Out of sight, Out of mind" is probably one of the most significant one you need to keep in mind to overcome procrastination. For a task to get executed it must be on top of your mind and in the line of your vision.

Going through the autobiography of Benjamin Roosevelt, I came to the piece where he describes his daily routine. One thing that caught my eye was what he did on coming back from work. After coming back and before relaxing, he would organize back the things he used to their designated place to ensure that they were found where they are supposed to be located. That small act itself if we do thoroughly can save us endless hours of search we waste looking for everyday things, the next morning. This brings us to the famous corollary of "A place for everything and everything in its place".

6 Not putting it on the calendar

Nature has a rhythm and we are all a part of it and the universal intelligence because of which the universe exists. Every day the sun rises and sets at about the same time. Seasons come and go cyclically. Similarly, our body clock also aligns with these cycles accordingly. We work during the day and sleep at night when our energy ebbs. It's another matter that we might have many variations in when we wake up and when we go to sleep. Similarly, our energy level is also dependent on when we eat and rest. We eat when we are hungry and rest when tired. However, the demands of modern life, takes a toll on these basic necessities. We eat when it's convenient and resting or relaxing is something we never seem to take seriously as something to be done at periodic intervals.

Similarly, what we do during the day is again a matter of our choice, habits and what we consider as important. Till the time a task has a proper starting and even an ending time, it would be at the mercy of our memory and the pressure of other competing tasks. Scheduling is thus one of the most overlooked activity we have to take to ensure that a task gets done. Until and unless a task is scheduled and there is an associated deadline, the scheduling is not complete. Even without a deadline, it is vitally important to schedule a task and then respect your decision by performing it at the assigned time.

Scheduling is not just an entry on the calendar but the entire preparation for doing it at the scheduled hour. It tells us what to do, how much to do, who can help, what else do we need and how much time is budgeted for it. Scheduling is something magical. It's as if you have put up a task at a certain time of the day which will take you ahead or may even change your life depending upon what you chose and what the outcome will be. The habit to schedule and then executing to completion what is planned can change your life completely.

7 The incessant battle with our heart

We look at work from *a cold state* and from there most of our doubts arise. A cold state is an off-work state when mentally we are disengaged to take up anything significant. Sitting in bed watching television is not an ideal state to ponder over a project report.

While some people might argue that that is the position where they can think better, but the fact remains that one is relatively much better off if they are ready in all sense of the word to tackle the issue at hand. Have you noticed that every significant work which nears conclusion gets into a climax and you are in frenzy? Things are happening left and right, deadlines drawing near and suddenly multiple things have to be wrapped up. You have to brace yourself up and that in turn changes the spirit with which you face the task at hand. On a normal day, getting a shower and changing into your outside clothes gets you into the state. Planning for the day, a few official calls and getting over with a small task can you put you in the right mindset to approach the day ahead in a battle-ready state. The bottom line is that nothing worthwhile gets done in a pajama suit except sleeping!

8 Getting our mind and heart to fall in line

Great things happen when our mind and heart are in sync with each other. But this is easier said than done. While our mind tells us that we have to finish a task, our heart has other ideas. Lack of focus is an outcome of an uncontrolled mind and a wavering heart.

A mind that is easily distracted and is prone to worries is soon overwhelmed by the work challenges and chaos around it and is soon in a state of emotional upheaval. A focused mind is set on a singular aim and more often than not achieves it. Biologically also we can only do justice to only one thing at a time. We have finite time and the industry of the world is limitless. You can't hope to excel at all or some of them. Why then focus be such an elusive fellow if it is under our command. This has to do with our mind not keeping still. If not focused it can run into various directions driven to our heart's desire. It also tends to achieve a state of lowest energy by just letting you remain in the comfort zone and avoid any risks. If you are used to keeping things steady and not do anything which makes you anxious, your mind may try to distract you to prevent completing the task which is the most important.

The present-day scenario has in fact compounded the problem with limitless knowledge available at the click of a button being available to us.

What sets the successful people out is not about what they know but how they apply when needed at the moment when it's required without any hang-ups and have unwavering focus despite the emotional upheavals their actions might bring. For them taking decisions on a daily basis is a way of life.

Soon the concentration locks in and one enters the zone in which magic is made and opportunities are converted into successful outcomes. Be at it and let the power of your focused mind convert into a fearless gladiator who has put to rest his fears and apprehensions and joined a cosmic force.

"Your chances of achieving a goal increases 10 times if you can hang on to it for the next 1 hour".

9 What seems like work...

You are your own biggest challenge. A victory over yourself is the first step to your success. Nothing, however, comes about if thoughts and plans are not converted into action. What separates winners from dreamers is their ability to take action small or big and keep moving forward. Anything before action does not add value. The world recognizes only this and *pays for it.*

Odds are stacked against an average person to make it big. Thousands are waiting with similar or better abilities to outpace and outbid you. However, your uniqueness along with your ability to take action will set you apart. Specific steps and tools are though required to convert thoughts into action until and unless you are driven by passion alone. I have a favorite saying that says that *"replace worry time by action time". This is because, once you take action, your focus changes from mulling over the bottlenecks to active possibilities. Once we are in motion, as per Newton's First law of Motion, the body continues to be in a state of motion.* Every venture presents risks, problems, and uncertainties but they will not come or become apparent at once. Cross bridges when you come to them. There is no point in just mulling over the risks and worry endlessly. Everything can be overcome if done the right way and on time. Seize the initiative and be a crusader. Show that you have the ability and ambition to do what it takes.

Many of us wait for the perfect moment to start. You may think like this, "The day when I will have a relaxing holiday is when I have the time and all the present worries or challenges I am facing are over". That day as you may notice never arrives. The one key skill that you have to learn to achieve what you have planned is to take action and become more productive. Productivity is about finishing what you started, with accuracy, timeliness and the desired quality. Get into the habit of completing things howsoever small that may be. It's not a productive habit to leave work incomplete.

A piece of pen and paper is the greatest aid to depict your thoughts into words and pictures. As a ground rule for playing this game, you have to execute what is scheduled. Remember this is a new way to lead your life. But it is still on paper, it has to be adopted by your mind as a way of executing things first and then the actual execution. Remember all the beautiful things that you can do if you finish the work on time. Let the time that you create for yourself be the reward.

One of the ways on how habits are formed is to look at your bad habits and look at how they were formed. They are also after all habits. Why we are more prone to adopt bad habits is very intriguing.

Is it that what we called as bad habits are actually not bad habits after all? According to common wisdom, anything that harms our body is a bad habit like for example, smoking and excess consumption of alcohol. Still, we do it! But, that's not the way it seems when we are indulging in it. Then what is the reason? One of the reasons is certainly because there is an addictive element involved. However, it's also a fascinating insight into what we automatically do without any stimuli. We can gladly watch endless episodes of a Netflix series rather than spending that time exercising, reading, playing with your kids or spending quality time with your spouse. Why is it so? The answer has partly to do with our awareness of choices we have, our sensitivity to use our time in a better way, our energy level and lack of a pull or a reason to choose a particular task over another.

Think about the last time you felt highly productive. You

probably had a sense of being in control, were not stressed out and were highly focused on the work at hand; time tended to disappear (lunchtime already?), and you felt you were making noticeable progress toward a meaningful outcome. If you are not in this state, then perhaps you are nowhere near completion.

Cultivate the habit of entering the productivity zone at will. This is one habit that will take you ahead of the competition. It is fascinating that when you study the most effective individuals throughout history you see the same theme coming back again and again in how each of them managed their time. The key was focus and concentration on a few very significant priorities; always keeping in mind what was centrally important at the moment.

Winston Churchill was the Prime Minister of the United Kingdom during the Second World war period from 1940-1945.

He died in 1965. Even then, he was voted as one of the "100 most influential Britons of all Time" in a BBC Poll held in 2002. He was at the first place of the ranking such was his impact even 37 years after his death!

Despite his wide-ranging attention and interests he always kept in mind what was centrally important to the moment – it was relentlessly focused upon it and would not be turned aside. Ultimately this served as the cornerstone of his time management system. His general method of work was to concentrate his personal attention on the two or three things that mattered the most and devote all the time and attention that they demanded.

Churchill was capable of tremendous physical and intellectual efforts of high intensity over long periods often with little sleep.

But at the same time, he had corresponding powers of relaxation filled with a variety of pleasurable occupations and he also had the gift of taking short naps when time permitted.

His success secret was to develop a daily schedule and routine for his personal time. He was totally organized almost like a clock. This routine was absolutely dictatorial. He set himself ruthless timetable every day and would get very agitated in case he was not able to follow it.

10 The epic struggle to go the entire distance

Notice what happens when a work is about to finish, especially a project. There is hectic activity and a lot of work is transacted at the eleventh hour. This is when things are reaching a climax. The climax is perhaps the biggest indicator that work is getting finished. If things have not reached a certain level of frenzy, then work completion is still some distance away. The climax is an important characteristic of any significant work and happens when we are committed to a close.

An Indian Wedding is a spectacle by itself. Preparation starts many months earlier with purchases for boy and the girl by opposite sides. Then, it calls for various arrangements in the form of bookings for the venue, managing various ceremonies and finally the wedding. There is a hectic last-minute activity with relations trooping in, deliveries, and logistics being taken care of. Finally, the wedding gets over early the next morning when finally the bride is given the farewell by the parents and relatives to be driven with the groom to her new abode. The activity reaches a feverish pitch before finally the end outcome is reached and the parents from both sides heave a collective sigh of relief. While the preparation for the wedding happens over a period of many months, it reaches a feverish pace and climaxes in the last few days of the wedding. Similarly, an important task or a project also reaches a climax just before its close. If the climax is missing then perhaps, you are still a long distance away from completion.

When work reaches a climax, it occupies more and more of our mind and workspace till it occupies centre stage. You may need to sacrifice a lot of things at this stage, your comfort, enjoyment, self and family time and a lot more. In short, a sacrifice is required. In the above example, the parents and the family of both the groom and the bride sacrifice their time, effort and money to make the grand event happen leaving no stone unturned to make it a great success.

Thus, if climax and sacrifice are not present together, then probably the work is still a long way from completion, or you may not have decided on taking the plunge completely.

Please understand that it's only action that makes the work move forward. Waiting, planning, organization without action is just a waste of time and is the road to oblivion. It might take a few hours or stretch your misery for years together!

11 The magic of completion

There is something magical about completion. Remember when you finished your senior school, college or finished reading a book. How did it feel? An incomplete task is like doing the task many times over. The next time you pick up an incomplete task you would have to overcome the dreaded starting potential. Every time you leave starting incomplete, the work potential starts increasing and soon it becomes as high as when it was initially started. The fact we are not able to complete tasks simply means that we are not able to enter our zone. Once we enter our productive zone, work starts moving quickly.

It's a habit that must be cultivated; working quickly does not leave space for thinking. This thinking should have been done a day before while creating the plan for the next day. Mixing execution with decision making will upset your rhythm and will lead to procrastination.

Completion very often happens because there is a deadline looming large or there are repercussions. If we are not meeting our goals, then probably we are not completing those small tasks and taking small actions that can take you nearer to them.

12 Going to the next level

Evolution is the law of life. To become better, to take it to the next level is a goal of any individual. Evolution is only possible when a basic version is ready or the boundaries are set. The dilemma is to see what is the level of perfection we want.

We have discussed all the important impediments and forces at work that stops our day from becoming a wishing well and keeps our success, happiness, prosperity, and productivity under leash. In the next chapter, we will discuss specific approaches, tips, and tricks to master the three "Value Destroyers" that we discussed. We will look at some of the key levers that we need to control to make our day productive also see some vital factors that lend balance and meaning to our life. We will also understand that one rule which governs any work that we do and is singlehandedly capable of helping us accomplish big changes that can change the course of our life. Finally, we will begin with the introduction of the twin frameworks that go hand in hand in making lending a structure to our day and enable us to handle all that life throws at us in-between.

THE KNOWLEDGE

Making it all Work Within a Day

"I have two kinds of problems, the urgent and the important.
The urgent are not important and the important are never urgent"
Dwight D Eisenhower

We have seen in the previous chapters how starting potential, noise and effectiveness destroyers have the potential to rob us of our powers and make us feel helpless in any endeavor. However, the effect of these factors can be minimized and even eliminated. What if we can devise a repeatable formula that kills these success limiters? In this, chapter we will discuss practices whose knowledge is fairly common but their application is not well understood. They, if pieced together form a framework that works like magic if practiced and habituated. Soon, a pattern starts appearing with which you can structure your day, control and execute the work that will fill it with.

In this chapter, I will introduce two frameworks; The Day Framework and the Effectiveness Framework (E-Framework). *The Day Framework* is about putting a structure around your day from the time you wake up to the time you hit the bed at night. This is the first framework to master. This framework itself might be sufficient to solve more than half of all your productivity and time management issues. It's simple and many of us follow it partially and sometimes fully. It will bring about positive changes in all areas of your life and you will have more energy and vitality to achieve all that you plan to do. While the Day Framework gives the structure to the day, the Effectiveness Framework is about handling all the work and other activities that you will plan within it. It provides an engine through which you can pass all your work. It consists of 12 elements divided into 4 verticals. Not all tasks require all the 12 elements it contains to be gone through. It can be used to handle all the incoming work which could include from simple tasks to your most cherished goal till the time they are completed and still can be evolved further However, before we move to these frameworks, let's try to understand what we want to achieve from a day.

4.1 THE SIX LEVERS TO CONTROL YOUR DAY

We as human beings have limited time on earth. Our day is locked up between essential, livelihood related and personal activities. Thus we have a limited time within which to work out miracles. How can we optimize the day to achieve our goals and dreams?

For this, we have to have a set of fundamental levers that we can use to govern our day and impact our goals one way or the other. We have at our disposal choices that we can use to manage ourselves but in the rigmarole of life, we hardly get into the practice of using them. What if we can whip out at will these tools to take control of the day? Let's look at these key control levers which we can exercise.

1 ABILITY TO CREATE SPACE

Creating more space is perhaps the biggest service you can do yourself and for your family and to your general well-being. Time, priorities, body and mind will always be falling out of tune with each other. Contrary to what intuition might tell you, time management is actually self-management, which in turn is about completing what is essential and also about keeping a balance between work and personal life. How many times have you exclaimed that, "if only I had more time", I would actually do things that I really like". However, in our day to day life, we seem to be running with our back to the wall and we forget to draw a line between public and private life. Imagine in this chaotic life we lead, we can completely detach ourselves and not do any work and then also nothing gets delayed. What if you can decide to suddenly have to take a day off and do nothing and still be in control? A planned day can afford you that luxury. You can pluck time at will and consume as and when you like. This makes this option an unexplainable luxury. This is a lever you can exercise to cut-off, step-back and re-think your approach and priorities. This can be valuable to actually decide if you want to go ahead with the planned action or you got to relax and re-plan the entire thing.

2 UNDERSTANDING AND EXECUTING OUR PRIORITIES

This is one thing that most people get wrong. Ask anyone what is important for them in life and the stock and generally honest answer is that it's their health, work, family, kids' future etc. After that ask them how they spend their day and most of the time the reply would be that it is their work that occupies the biggest slice of the day. Once that realization dawns, the concept of balance is gone. You may earn money but will not have time to spend it. You may have the most modern luxuries but won't have the looks, health or time to enjoy them. The whole day will then be a fuzzy cloud of work which leaves you breathless and dissatisfied.

In our day to day life, we are so embroiled in a plethora of activity around us, that we easily lose sight of what's important for us. One of the biggest victim of this is our health. Stories are legion of how people in their quest to earn money and fame spoiled their health almost permanently. From there on, though one has fame and money, health is no longer the same and requires constant attention and medication. Modern life also takes a heavy toll of our family time. We simply take family time as disposable time and easily trade it for other pursuits. The list of things we do in lieu of what's essential will amaze you and maybe make you also introspect.

We will show later that executing around priorities is nether difficult or time consuming. Key actions take a fraction of the time compared to what we spend in deciding, waiting for the right moment, or doing things in an unproductive way. You can achieve major goals if you can segregate the noise surrounding you and identify those key value-added actions that take very little time so as to squeeze them during your work day itself.

3 ISOLATING SIGNAL FROM THE NOISE THAT SURROUNDS US

Noise is all that does not let you focus on your Signal i.e. Goals and what is important for you. *Signal to Noise ratio* is a term used describing the strength of a signal compared to the background noise. Greater the ratio, greater is the signal compared to the background noise.

Noise, as we read earlier, stands between your success day in and day out. Don't let the trivia (noise) mask what is important i.e. the Signal. The ultimate outcome is stress which is like the sweat of modern life. The work we do leaves us stressed. Stress is the constant anxiety to achieve and feeling guilty if you are sitting free. The Master of the Day regimen puts you in the commander seat through which you can execute, monitor your day to day work and make changes if events happen not as anticipated. Managing noise will keep you going even under pressure and also help execute better.

4 BECOMING PRODUCTIVE

To be able to focus all our attention and focus on one task and to be able to take the most optimal task to completion is very often the result of planning and developing a methodology to perform work. There are different ways to achieve the same outcome. The difference is the time, effort, and finally the quality of the outcome. In your case, it means that it will take that much longer to optimize what you have achieved and get the true potential of the opportunity. To be able to find the most optimal way of doing the job and execute accordingly is another lever that you can use to control your day.

5 BECOMING PROACTIVE

Being proactive means to be able to view work linked up in the near future and acting upon it. This really liberates you and creates the space that you crave for. So much of the last-minute rush can be avoided if we can reach the desired outcome earlier and with less stress. The proactive mode is the best way to handle small tasks as they have a tendency to get into an urgent mode and trip over your priorities when they boil over. To anticipate events is great but to act proactively on them will put you into a different league.

6 CREATING BALANCE

Balance is about paying proportionate if not equal attention to various parts of your life important for your well-being during the course of the day. The most notable areas are self, family, health, and money. Keeping all these aspects into mind requires planning, discipline, and energy. To be able to create a balance is not easy but we shall see in the next section it is not difficult either. You can achieve a lot within a day; in fact, you can change your life in a day if you want to!

The 6 Levers are what we will address in the coming chapters to act as guideposts to manage our day.

4.2 THE VITAL 4 ELEMENTS IN OUR LIFE

So what is it if we were to become the Master of the Day we may like to achieve? At a very basic level

1. *We want to remain healthy*

2. *We want to be happy*

3. *We want to become better at what we do.*

4. *We want to prosper*

These are the big categories which we all aspire to have but never seem to be able to work concertedly. But, make no mistake, you can ignore but cannot avoid these if you want to strike a balance in your life. They form the essence of your existence.

Can we achieve all this in the space of a day? Yes, you can! It's just a matter of perception. As I will show below there are is sufficient time during the day to achieve all this and a lot more.

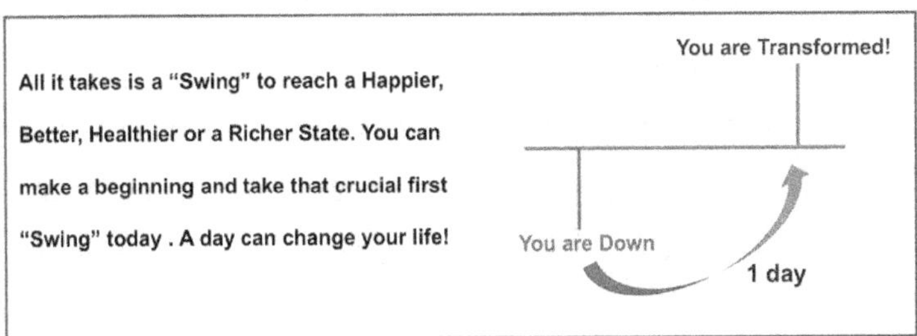

1 BEING HEALTHIER

It is ironical that we buy bad health at a premium. That extra juicy cheeseburger, drinking binges or that generous helping of a cake may seem to satiate our cravings and provide nirvana to six inches of distance through which food travels from our mouth to our gullet and makes our taste buds dance with joy and pass happy messages to our brain. But once the food is down our gullet, the reality unfolds when the food is broken into fats, carbohydrates or proteins and other constituents. This is what really counts in our body! Unfortunately, this is not the way it seems to us. What is sensed is what our mind believes and craves for!

Here are a few things you can do to get your thought process started.

- Beginning today you can *choose* to have healthy options on your plate and simply purge any thought to have any junk food.
- You can spend say 30 minutes doing meditation or mindfulness activities
- You can run / exercise at the gym for one hour.
- Have a game of tennis, badminton, football or any other sport for 1 hour.
- Read books and articles about diet, lifestyle and their impact on our body for just 15 minutes or more. Reading magnetizes you for change.

You can pick and choose out of the above and assign a slot for them during the day and if not possible daily, then during the week.

2 BEING HAPPIER

When was the last time you were happy, really happy? You might find this incredulous and think, "I am doing fine", "I am in fact quite happy". But by happiness I mean, being happy as a child with not a care in the world or that feeling of exultation that you felt when you won in a team sport or in an individual event. Happiness is our natural state. If we purge all thoughts or move away to a place where we cannot act on our worries, then very soon we end up a happy state. Thus, if we peel off layers of worry, distractions, looping thoughts and just relax, you will immediately feel happier. Some of the things that we can do during the day to become happier are:

- Play with your child or plan an outing with your family for a few hours over the weekend.
- Spend half an hour reading a good book and soaking in the story or trying to see how you can use the tips provided in the self-help book in your daily routine.
- Decide that you will not berate yourself, rather praise yourself and not worry even one bit for 1 hour. See the difference afterward. Increase the duration gradually.
- Spend 15 minutes doing gardening, tending to your indoor or outdoor plants or any other hobby whatever that may be. Point is to immerse yourself in the activity and purge any distracting thoughts during that time.
- The present age is about narcissism. Social media like Facebook, Instagram, and YouTube have stoked the need even more. Being self-obsessed is a one way street to misery and it has no destination. To get out of this try your hand at a charity. This first of all will be a reality check on how

fortunate you are and the fact that you can make a positive contribution to improving someone's life and will take your mind off your self-obsession. Charity work can range from helping someone in need and arranging for the needs of a person who needs medical help, doing part-time contribution at a charitable center or teach an illiterate person. Plan to spend a few hours on this over a period of one month.

3 BECOMING BETTER

Our mind is a super-computer and it can be taught or it can be used to become better at anything we do. But, very often we stop learning after reaching a comfortable position. Becoming better is about finding more meaning in what you presently do. While you can become better at many things but from the context of managing your day, you can become faster, more productive and decisive.

Here are a few ideas which you can consider or you can identify your own needs and start working on them.

- Join an online course to add a qualification or learn a new concept.
- Write a diary for 30 minutes reflecting on what went right, what went wrong and lessons learnt.
- Pick up an important task you have been procrastinating on and start working on it immediately.
- Spend an hour or more retraining yourself or learning a new skill.
- Execute several steps that take you nearer to your cherished goal.

- Complete at least ten 2-minute tasks that you had been putting away for months.
- You can schedule or have that all-important but contentious meeting that will help solve an issue.
- If you are job-hunting apply for at least 5 online jobs within a space of 1 hour.
- You can make at least 10 calls which matter.
- You can contact a mentor and schedule a meeting that can change your life.

4 BECOMING RICHER

Remember the money and time equation we delved on in Chapter 2? As we saw that money is what oils our existence in the civilized world. Only by developing an understanding about how money is earned and retained can we become richer. Just working for a pay cheque at the end of the month and not making any effort to become more educated or taking any action leading to earning more of it is a sign that you will struggle financially. However, in our daily life we just about manage to do all things lined up before us and we tend to forget that our workday is basically governed by the need to earn money. Thus, thinking and devoting time to what we are earning, how to maximize it and how to earn more of it in different ways is something we must inculcate. Here are a few activities that will get you started on your road to "money consciousness". For making them work, you have to bake them into your daily routine.

- Tracking your expenses and noting them down is the first step in ensuring that we start becoming conscious about how we spend money and also helps us check where we are overspending. Do this every day for 15 minutes.

- Maintain a budget consisting of essential categories into which you can divide your spending. A budget is what will keep your expenses in check and will lead to healthy saving habits ultimately. Review your budget status at least weekly to ensure that your spending doesn't cross your earnings and you have a "net profit" at the end of the month.

- Once you have the above two practices in place, the resultant savings must be put to good use in investments rather than putting them into a low interest earning savings bank account.

- Take the first step towards financial independence by setting your financial goals and how you will achieve them. Spend 1 hour to start researching your next investment.

- Join a course or start reading about money to develop your financial IQ. The more you become adept at thinking about money, the lesser will be your struggle to earn, retain and grow it.

The Vital 4, if programmed into you day will definitely inculcate a feeling of well-being and fulfillment .Here is an exercise to get you started immediately.

Exercise: *Create your own list of what you would like to do under each of these categories. Take your time and think about each of* *them deeply. Not all the activities need to be performed daily else there may be too many of them to handle. Stagger them over a week or a month to space them out. Doing these is linked to your sense of balance and overall well-being don't neglect it.*

4.3 THE 5% RULE

All work that we do is made of processes or a series of activities. Work is a sequence of activities which if completed converts inputs into outputs. A project or a goal achievement also goes through a process. However, all processes are affected by wastes, starting potential and noise which obstruct the flow of the work and "kill" value. It is estimated that up to 95% of the work that we do does not add any value to what we are striving to achieve. Here is where you need to understand a very important concept of Value addition.

A. *Anything that takes us nearer to our goal is a "Value Add" and rest all is a "Waste". If you scroll back to the Vital 4 you will realize that they are all "value-added" activities and they take very little time.*

B. *Out of the total time realized in achieving a project or a goal, the value-added activities take very little time and can be lined up during the day.*

Additionally, all work that we do has an end consumer. It could be your business customer, your boss, your family, friend or it could even be you. The plain fact is the value lies in the eyes of the beholder. If the customer determines that an activity adds value to the final product/service; it's a "Value Add". Everything else is "Non-Value Add" and thus a waste. Being productive means to eliminate the non-value added activities, wastes, noise and starting potential to provide value in the least possible time. The longer it takes, more will be the cost in terms of money, stress and will delay your success.

If we purely act on the 'Value Added' activities during the day we can by implication increase our productivity by a whopping amount.

Let's say you want to change your job, how much time does getting a job take? Sometimes, there is so much inertia around this that many people dread the prospect of looking for a better paying and more satisfying one. Why is it so? First of all it brings out all the issues that you were sleeping on or pretending they didn't exist. It might be that your skills have become a jaded or don't have a clear market. A job process begins with looking for opportunities, selection, customization of existing resume and then applying on the job portal or directly to the employer. Sometime several weeks may pass before you are called or may never be called at all. Then the interview process may run into several rounds over several weeks and the final decision also may take some time. This cycle you have to repeat with several employers before you can close and land a job. On an average, a normal executive level application-hire cycle might take 8-10 weeks.

Now compare this to a scenario where you are being referred by someone in an organisation for a particular role. Instantly, you cut down several weeks of the process as you get direct access and may even have the interviews scheduled in proximity to each other quickly. This brings down the wastes and overall cycle time to 3-5 weeks.

Imagine a third scenario where you end up meeting a CEO of a company at a Golf course. You play nice golf. He likes your game and afterwards you end up discussing what you do over coffee. He likes your ideas and offers you to come over to his office tomorrow for a discussion. He makes you meet some senior managers on the spot, they provide their feedback and soon you get a call from HR to discuss the salary package. You have landed a new job, in the space of a few days only!

This example might be a bit farfetched but it makes an important observation about the actual time taken for getting a job closed. Overall, if you put all the interviews, discussions, negotiations they would hardly make for 8-10 hours while the entire end to end process took several weeks. So, theoretically, you could land a job even in one day! The rest of the time wherein you were waiting for a call, interviews and all other activities that could have taken place had you applied through a normal job portal or direct application had no value for you. As you can easily guess the total value-added time will be less than 5% of the overall time it took

Similarly, you may avoid going to the doctor to show a niggling back pain and after unsuccessful attempts at self-medication, you decide to meet the demon. The visit to the doctor may take 1-2 hours depending upon the commuting time but to make that visit you might have dithered over one week. This basically means that rest of the time is consumed in waiting for something, making decisions, looking for things, leaving and forgetting the work altogether and a range of various other reasons. Rough math will tell you the percentage of the value added time was again less than 5% of the total time taken.

4.4 THE DAY FRAMEWORK

For starting a journey, we have to know where are and what are the benefits of that journey. If we really want to capture a day, then we have to understand certain characteristics of our day and how we are placed vis a vis these phases. The first step is to structure your day into phases or zones and assign definite boundaries, clearly demarcated changeovers and timelines for certain fixed events associated with our daily existence. This is the container within which your daily routine will flow. This framework by itself is a complete time management routine. This will be the first level of your mastery.

The Day Framework is a set of levels we can consider like the many floors of a building. The difference here is that we start from the top of the building (i.e. the morning) and slowly descend down floor by floor. With this in mind, the following structure describes an illustrative model for dividing our day into different zones within which we can plan and execute our work and achieve the elusive "balance" that we seek in our life.

You must have seen a house or a building being constructed. It follows all the logical engineering detailing that you can think of. To bear the weight of the structure, the foundation is designed accordingly. The framework of the structure is put in place gradually floor by floor. Once the basic masonry and structural part are over, all the utilities and other facilities are put in place.

Finally, you are ready to move in. Similarly, you have to lay the structure of the day and then fill in your activities in the structure that you will perform during the day. These tasks may range in duration from as low as a few seconds to several hours. Some activities or series of activities responsible for creating the desired outcome may go on over several weeks, months or years.

If we want to be the "Master of the Day" then this is the first framework that has to be mastered. Decide now and commit to it! The phases of a day can be considered to be floors of a three-story house with the following layout. Consider your day to be starting from the top floor as you descend floor by floor.

The Third Floor can be considered to be the morning period, which is perhaps the most important and vital part of the day which many of us miss out on. Our work then takes over till the evening when finally we head for home. From sunrise, till we start our commute to reach our workplace, is the time when have still not begun work. We maybe just sleeping, getting ready or simply relaxing before the madness of the day takes over. This is our personal time when we are the brightest and the most energetic. This is also the time to work on something creative or something which requires your utmost concentration. You can achieve this all. Thus, it won't be inappropriate to call this time of the day as the "Golden Hours". We can change our life in these hours and achieve amazing productivity. Every moment in these Golden Hours are truly golden.

The Flight of Stairs: To get to the second floor you would need to go down a flight of stairs. In real terms, this means a changeover from personal space to public (work) space and we must prepare for it in the form of grooming, preparing, organizing and finally commuting to work. This is the first changeover in the day and a change in our mental state is required.

The Second Floor is the time when we are at work. The time normally between 9 AM to 5 PM wherein most of the people are engaged in doing some activity or the other is the "Productivity Zone". This is the work zone that consumes a major part of our "Up-time". What we do in these hours determine whether we will end up healthier, happier, better and richer at the end of the day. However, if we have not planned for it, we are likely to waste a major part of it. Again this is not the time you organize things, take decisions or get clarifications. You can work smarter if you dedicate this day to pure action fuelled by plan, decisions, and organization. A planned and focused day can change your life.

Just prior to the next changeover, we have to do the MOD planning for the next day. This is a critical activity you need to do for about 30 minutes or lesser and then fold-up

The Flight of Stairs: To get to the first floor we have to again go down a flight of stairs to reach the first floor. This is again a changeover period. However, as we will see later, here is where you will lay the seeds for the Mastery of Tomorrow i.e. the next day.

The First Floor: This signifies the evening. The time from evening till bedtime when most of us go back and relax or do some personal tasks is the final phase of our active time when we are back at home or out of work. This is the Post-Work or Personal Zone. This is the final floor we descend before we go to bed. The lifecycle of the day comes to an end when we retire to bed and go to sleep.

The ground floor can be considered to be the time when we sleep during the night, re-energising for the next day.

This is the natural framework within which a day unfolds. The Master of the Day at the very basic level is about aligning to the natural phases of the day before we even talk of things like capturing, deciding and executing work within the workday. The Master of the Day "Level One" is the day framework or structure in which your entire day's activities can be organized. This framework is the high-level demarcation of the phases in a day for you to operate. The timelines for this framework is the first objective we have to meet. But before that, we will have to measure where we are. This structure by itself is the first step towards effectively using our day and correcting our life. Only when you strike a rhythm in following this framework, will your life begin to change and be ready to take up responsibility.

From a work perspective, the zones may vary from person to person based on their work nature and timings. Many of us struggle with differentiating these three natural partitions of a day with the work aspect spilling over late into the evening. Morning time is lost altogether if we don't have a regular sleeping time. These zones have their own special characteristics and depending on your bio-rhythm you will need to plan your zones accordingly.

The Framework given below gives the contours of the day with changeovers. You have essentially two sleep events (waking-up and sleeping), three eating events (breakfast, lunch, and dinner) and two changeover events (going to work and coming back from work). This is not including an afternoon nap or additional meals you may take. These events can again vary between a weekday and a weekend. Some other terms that need to be understood are given below.

Golden Hours: These are the early morning hours when your mind is at the best in terms of focus, freshness. Aim for a 4:00 AM wakeup time or begin with 5:00 AM and gradually working towards the ideal wake-up time. This is the best time to do something creative or apply your mind to something complex. You will find that your productivity would be amazing during this time.

Changeovers: Changeovers are the specific time where you change gears during the day. The first changeover is in the morning before you begin your workday at your place of work. Here you will be entering public space from your personal space. The second major changeover is in the evening when you stop working and head home. Here you will be leaving public or professional space to go back to your personal space. Changeover means completely switching off from the previous phase or zone.

The figure below depicts the various zones including Golden Hours, Changeovers and Meals which together forms the "Day Framework".

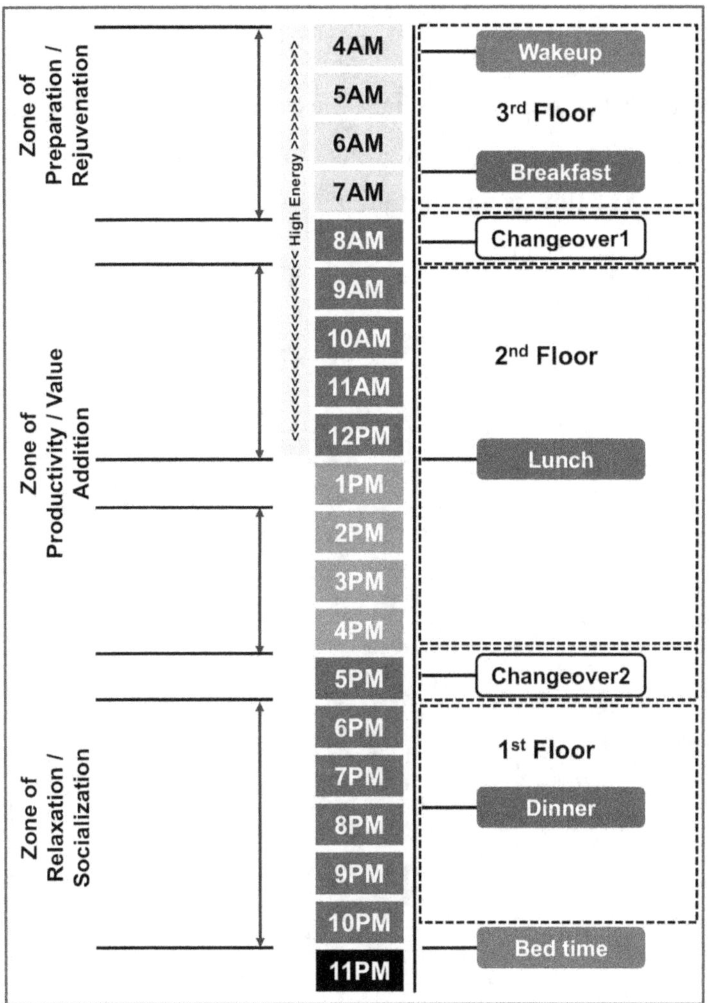

THE DAILY FRAMEWORK ESSENTIALS

Decide the three zones for yourself based upon your work timings. Maintaining these important timings will be the key to becoming the master of the day. If you can define your waking up time, your bedtime, leaving for work time, getting up from work time, this itself will be a huge step you would take towards claiming your day. Plan for the changeover timings. Apart from this, if you can further define your meal timings, you can immediately take a huge step towards regaining your health or improving upon it.

Given below is an illustration of where we are in terms of following a fixed routine.

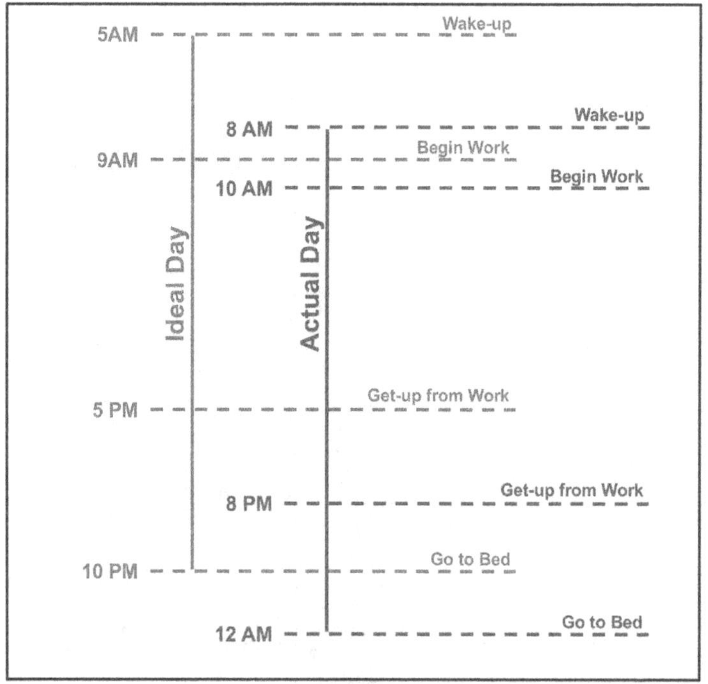

Out of the two possible frameworks which is the one your day closely resembles? In reality, the "Actual Day" framework shown above is very common and is the result of the lifestyle we lead in today's times. This shift is our first challenge. As you may have guessed MOD framework is based on the "Ideal framework".

These timings are however just illustrative and may vary slightly from person to person.

The work zone may have different content or meaning based upon the person's work nature.

- For an executive at work, it means attending meetings, working on projects, answering emails, meeting clients, etc.
- For a housewife, a day is filled with various household chores which may not change at all even over weekends.
- For a shop owner, it's about running the day to day affairs manage customers, calling up suppliers, or manage the shop.
- For a worker, it's about doing a shift and being engaged in primarily one type of work only.

Thus, most of our working time during the day is locked or committed in activities and thus leaves early mornings, evenings and weekends only at our disposal.

BENJAMIN FRANKLIN

If ever there was this mythical, "Jack of All Trades", it had to be Benjamin Franklin, who was one of the founding fathers of America. In his life, he traversed an astounding range of roles and professions which is well beyond comprehension and he achieved all this within a lifetime and with the same daily hours which every average living person is blessed with. Benjamin Franklin was an author, politician, thinker, scientist, postmaster, inventor, printer, writer, herb-doctor, statesman, orator, diplomat and much more.

How in the world a man can achieve all this in his lifetime? While no doubt he was a genius but so many other geniuses that we have known from history were able to impact one particular area but his resume reads like a bewildering collection of careers which would befit a dozen other geniuses all put together. How did he achieve all this? From what we know of him, he was an astutely disciplined man and religiously followed his daily routine. The foundation of his time management was based on the thirteen values that he famously ingrained in himself one by one tirelessly, one at a time and worked on mastering them towards guiding his daily discourse and use as a moral compass in case he went astray. The 13 values are Temperance (eat not to dullness), Silence(speak only what will benefit others), Order (let all things have their designated place), Resolution (perform without fail what you resolve), Frugality(waste nothing), Industry (lose no time),sincerity(use no hurtful deceit), Justice (wrong no one), moderation (avoid extremes), cleanliness (keep self and surroundings clean), tranquillity(don't let minor issues bother you), chastity (over sexual indulgence), humility(imitate the lives of great people).Sample some of these values and you would come across tenets of astute time management and a peep into the practices that made this man destined for greatness. Through "order" he ordained to keep objects of use at their appointed place and assign tasks and activities to a particular time slot in his daily routine. Once scheduled he carried them out religiously without fail. This was also apparent in his definition of the value of "Resolution ". In following the value of "Industry", he professed that time to him was a quantity not to be lost in unnecessary activities and he lost no time doing them. To avoid distractions he maintained the value of "silence" and only spoke if it benefitted others and avoided mindless gossip. Thus, these values all 13 of them acted as beacons that guided his lifeboat. Apart from this, all this can only be managed through immaculate record keeping and thus he kept a diary to track his compliance with his beloved values and managing his affairs of the day. His day was divided into predefined intervals in which he kept time to work, relax and most importantly observe and reflect on his performance. His daily schedule started with a resolution on what good he shall do today and his day ended with a review of what good he accomplished and self-examination.

The morning time which started with his waking up at 4 AM, he reserved for meditation and planning for the day to follow and perform the main area of study he was engaged in at that point. Once at work he would spend straight four hours working before taking a break for food and also have a quick look at his finances.

His day ended with self-examination, putting things in their order and then followed by dinner and some unwinding activity like music or light conversation before retiring to bed at around 10 PM and waking up again at 4 AM. Benjamin Franklin embodied all the concepts taught in this book and has been an inspiration for millions of others who continue to be astonished at what he could achieve.

Let's look at the phases of the day and see how they can be tuned to create something that each one of us can adapt on a day to day basis to manage our daily routine better. For us to function effectively these three zones have an important role to play but we also have to ensure that boundaries of these phases are not violated.

To begin defining your day will be a small step towards starting to define your life. Nothing in this life comes easy. Years of not adhering to proper work and personal space will make it difficult to accept that the time for work is over or it's time to go to bed. However, if you persist, they will become your new habits and soon you will start noticing that your life is changing for the better.

It's not easy to change though. There is always a tendency to send that last e-mail or make a call, or catch that extra sleep in the morning. The biggest sufferer in this matter is the overall sleep time. Lack of sleep can derail the "Master of the Day" routine. It won't be inappropriate to say that it hinges on this aspect. Sleep is like the fueling up time. What happens when despite your body signals you are not going to sleep? You end up creating a situation wherein the effects of it are seen the next morning and the whole day through. You are tired, unfocussed and depleted. What good is that?

Apart from this, not following a fixed routine makes your time susceptible to anything that occupies your mind or attention. If not controlled your schedules can fluctuate like a yo-yo. Your body then can never fall into a rhythm. Given below is an illustrative framework with activities filling up the various phases.

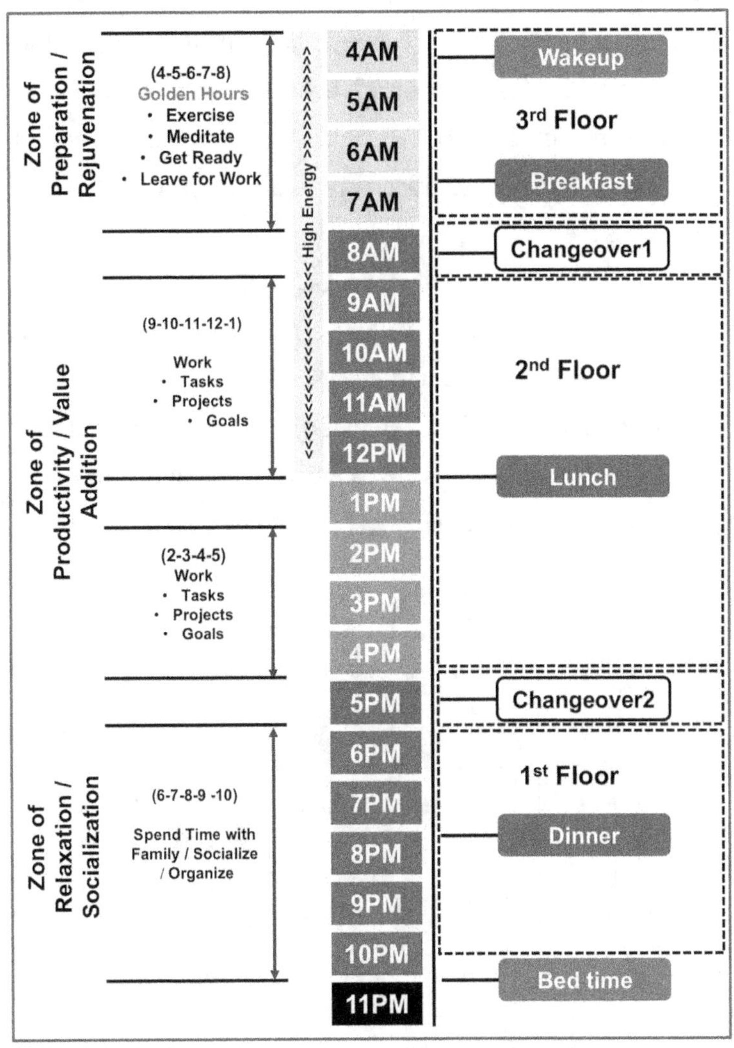
Zone of Preparation / Rejuvenation
(4-5-6-7-8)
Golden Hours
• Exercise
• Meditate
• Get Ready
• Leave for Work
High Energy
Zone of Productivity / Value Addition
(9-10-11-12-1)
Work
• Tasks
• Projects
• Goals
(2-3-4-5)
Work
• Tasks
• Projects
• Goals
Zone of Relaxation / Socialization
(6-7-8-9 -10)
Spend Time with Family / Socialize / Organize
4AM
5AM
6AM
7AM
8AM
9AM
10AM
11AM
12PM
1PM
2PM
3PM
4PM
5PM
6PM
7PM
8PM
9PM
10PM
11PM
Wakeup
3rd Floor
Breakfast
Changeover1
2nd Floor
Lunch
Changeover2
1st Floor
Dinner
Bed time

4.5 THE EFFECTIVENESS FRAMEWORK (E-FRAMEWORK)

Once the Daily Framework has been laid out and habituated we can move to a framework or a process through which we can execute work within the day. This is the second framework we will introduce to tackle all the tasks, projects and achieve the 'Vital 4'. We call this the Effectiveness Framework (E-Framework). It takes into account all the levers that we discussed and then eliminates starting potential, wastes and all the effectiveness destroyers that rob our day from us. We will discuss all these elements of the E-Framework in more detail. Here is a quick summary of each of the listed elements. Not all the elements are required depending upon work type and complexity.

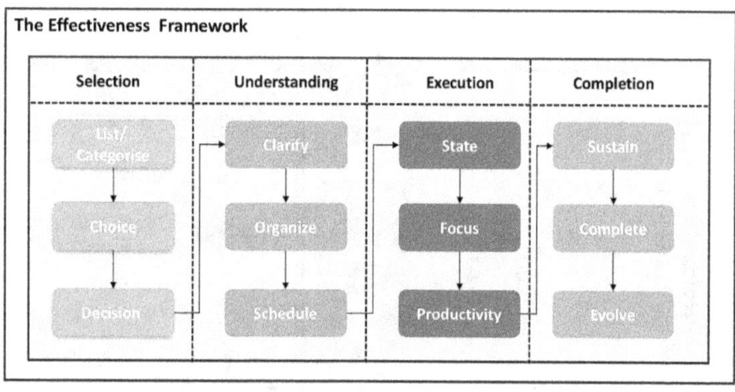

1. List/Categorize is about capturing the incoming work, listing, screening and categorizing them. The list may exist on paper or may just be in your mind.

2. The choice is about what you choose to work on priority. We make choices every moment consciously or subconsciously.

These choices determine what outcomes we observe in our life. The matter of choice does not just extend to our physical actions but also to what we choose to think.

3. The decision is about taking a call if you will indeed go through the motions and are convinced that this is the outcome that is required and will stick to it. In reality, we are not fully convinced about many things and the end result is that we keep thinking about but don't act upon it. Making a decision could be the most liberating feeling after which the starting potential reduces dramatically.

4. Clarity is about what is needed to accomplish a goal or an outcome. Sometimes all we have is a wish. For example, we may wish to join an elite college or want to become rich. These are by themselves bulk and vague goals. Left to themselves they would never be achieved. Getting clarity is about understanding what it takes to reach a goal either by self-education, or by speaking to someone who has done it before or by hiring a professional person to guide or do the work for you.

5. A habit to keep things organized will reduce your wasted efforts looking for things, revisiting and remembering about work done earlier.

6. The schedule is about putting the tasks in a particular prioritized sequence on a calendar. Only tasks that are scheduled have a realistic chance of getting done on time.

7. The state is about your getting into a position of physical readiness and mental agility required to do a particular task.

The ideal condition to achieve is that of a flow when you are in your deep productive zone when you are intensely focusing on the work and taking it to completion and all the noise in the background becomes a blur.

8. Focus is about the centeredness which enables you to focus on only one thing at a time allotted for it. Focusing on many things will leave you tired and frustrated.

9. Productivity is about doing a task in the most optimal way and leading it to a close in the shortest possible time. Until and unless we are working as a worker in a factory, we are not primed to work optimally. Productivity is also about being able to do what matters and which is seen as adding value in the eyes of the people who are depending on you including yourself.

10. Sustain consists of two important elements viz. the climax and the sacrifice. The climax is about the final stage at which the work reaches its feverish pace full of ups and downs and final victory. Anything worthwhile that you wish to achieve will reach that stage. If there is no climax involved then probably your work/goal is still far from the finishing line. Sacrifice is about the compromise you have to make to achieve a certain work/goal at the expense of leaving other tasks, relaxation or other any other activity which may tempt you.

11. Complete is about taking the work to the final stage. Only completed work has any value in your life and is the one that the world recognizes and is willing to pay for.

12. Evolve is the stage when your work has taken shape and

now you can take it to the next level. This is a stage when your mind is free from the work done and you can focus on the value add or improvement that you were not able to do earlier being engrossed in finishing the work.

4.6 THE E-FRAMEWORK AS A PROCESS

This is the basic process that comes out of the E-framework. It has all it takes to manage, process and complete incoming work and even beyond it. As we go through each of the elements in detail in the subsequent sections, try visualizing taking all your work through this process all the time. Soon this will be ingrained in your mind and then can be applied automatically. However, the process may not be applicable for all types of work. Simple tasks may just need to be scheduled and executed. Thus, this process is an engine that is customizable depending upon your needs.

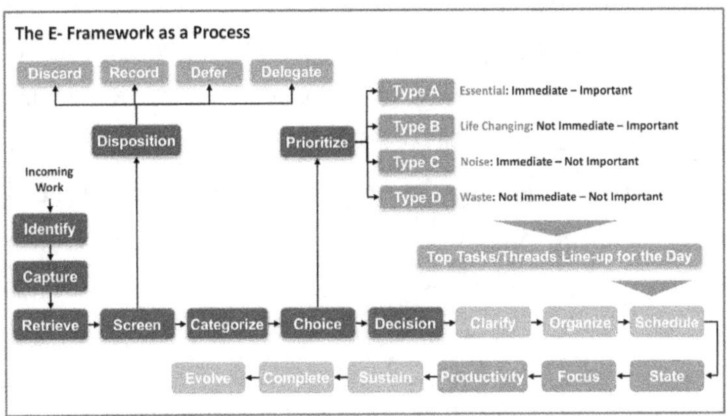

The process lays the E-Framework as a series of steps from work identification to completion and further evolution. As you can see anytime we are just moving from one step to the other, we are just waiting and not adding any value. The steps are the "Value Adds". As an exercise, just note down how much time a work identified took from identification to completion. You will surely realize the time that it took was significantly more than the total time it took to go through all the steps taken together. The List / Categorize element have a few additional steps to identify, capture, retrieve, screen the incoming work. Thus screening is the first level qualification of incoming work where the decision regarding its treatment is taken. This step itself removes a lot of noise entering our work categories as will see shortly. Similarly the Choice step depicts the work prioritization approach which we will explain in the next chapter.

The Selection and Understanding verticals have to be executed at the planning and review stage itself i.e. during the MOD planning for the next day.

In the next chapter, we will look at the first two verticals of the E-Framework i.e. Selection and Understanding. Remember that each of these elements is a complete subject by itself so the effort will be to keep things simple and use them more consciously while handling work. Slowly, you will start using them without even being conscious of their usage.

E-Framework – Selection & Understanding

5.1 INTRODUCTION

Selection and Understanding of work coming to us is not given the due importance it deserves as all our efforts are directed towards execution. However, even before execution starts we have to line-up, understand and make the work ready for execution. To enable smooth and optimal execution we have to ideally undergo a series of systematic steps to ensure that all the incoming work is properly screened, selected, understood and finally scheduled for action. The first two verticals of the E-Framework explain the selection and understanding process. They both have three elements each which are explained in detail in this chapter.

5.2 LIST / CATEGORIZE

This is the most basic but incredibly powerful tool to capture the work coming to you from various mediums. We will start with the collection of all the tasks and projects that you have and putting them all together in a list called simply as a Work list. We will discuss the mechanism to capture incoming work a bit later. You may have more creative ideas about naming the sheet as a "To Do", "My Activity List", " Win List" or something zany as " The Game List" if you are gaming enthusiast and can visualize finishing the tasks for the day as a score in a game. Reframing our situation alters our perspective and makes us much more likely to finish the tasks at hand. So whatever motivates you should be your terminology.

Work list by its very nature may tend to be infinite and then maybe you shouldn't mind that. Making a work list is not only about listing the work to be done but also about identifying work that you can leave alone for a while, delegate or even eliminate altogether.

The work list is a collection of all the work that you have to decide upon to ensure you lead an effective and peaceful life in congruence with your goals and work demands. The idea is not to get sucked into a never-ending spiral of work. Rather, it is an effort to capture what needs to be done to ensure that you manage the trivial and focus on the vital, without letting the trivial getting into the way every now and then. The work list is not about creating an endless list of work to be done. This itself will add to your stress. The work list is supposed to de-stress you by keeping you focused on key tasks that are aligned to your priority and goals.

The work-list is also about facing responsibility. Once you have identified tasks that are on priority, executing them will mean that you have to come out of your comfort zone. Take your priority task or project and try going systematically through the steps until it reaches the completion stage.

Have a complete listing ensuring that you empty all the things from your memory onto a physical and permanent medium which can be accessed again so you won't have to worry about forgetting an urgent task altogether or take your eyes off certain tasks which if not acted upon now can result in a missed deadline or it becoming urgent and tripping off the more important tasks that had on your schedule.

Also, remember that a vast majority of people do manage without any checklists and there is a fine line between being extremely structured and madness. If this practice does not make you visibly more organized and effective than the people around you then stop and analyze as to why it's not working. You may only be creating lists without taking them further for processing and completion.

Our mind is fickle and has temporary power to process things parallelly. To put it simply it is not meant for multi-tasking like a computer. Multi-tasking in the case of human beings can at best be multiple tasks executed one after the other sequentially. This often turns out to be counterproductive as all tasks take different time to complete and if there is no prioritization; we may end up wasting time on unimportant but urgent tasks.

Given below is a general methodology for the List / categorize step.

5.2.1 METHODOLOGY

STEP 1: IDENTIFY

At this moment work is either lying undocumented, in your mind or entering through the inflow mechanisms like e-mails, verbally from people or self-generated.

STEP 2: CAPTURE

For this, you must have a way or series of ways to capture the work as it occurs and record it. All these streams must ultimately coalesce into one place (either in your diary, phone or laptop). Capture the work as it occurs to you that very moment before it goes out of memory. The problem lies in capturing work as and when it comes to us through a reliable process which takes into account your state of preoccupation at that moment, your capture method and a visibility cue to remind you of the task. Identify all the work listed in a diary/notebook, computer or your smartphone. It's important to list down the work howsoever small it may be.

You can use various mediums to capture work as it occurs to you. With the continuous advancement of smartphone capabilities, you have a tool in hand to capture work in sheets, productivity apps like Evernote or simply as a voice message if you happen to be driving. What happens when the work occurs to you when you are taking bath or in a place where you have no means to capture? In these cases, it is best to write down the tasks at the earliest when you can.

STEP 3: RETRIEVE

Retrieve the work you have captured and then work on it further. Visibility is a critical factor. Whatever is out of sight is likely to be out of mind too. If the work is in front of you, the probability of it getting done increases dramatically. The initial work list may just be an unsorted list having all tasks and projects listed as they come to your mind. You need to have a single source where you can see all your work listed, sorted and prioritized. If this is not the case, the starting potential will increase and soon you will forget even about the work list itself.

STEP 4: SCREEN INCOMING WORK

The next step consists of screening the potential work you have listed. You have the following options before you at this stage. The work can be eliminated, deferred, executed or delegated.

▶ **Discard:** Not every work needs to be done. Similarly, you can analyze from which source a lot of non-value add tasks are coming and needs to be stopped. Try to eliminate incoming work by acting on the origination source itself putting mechanisms to stop or manage that work without having to get involved.

▶ **Record:** Some of the work coming into your daily routine may just be purely information like a date for a meeting or a newsletter that needs to be read. They simply need to be entered in your calendar as an entry or as a "to read" item.

▶ **Defer:** This is about putting off work depending upon its priority. Scheduling to read a book which you have just bought in the coming holidays or scheduling to complete a task the deadline for which is still far away at a future time are some of the examples of deferred work.

▶ **Delegate:** This is the work that you have decided to give to your team member, family member or even to a friend. This act frees up your time for more productive pursuits.

A lot of work coming our way can be eliminated once we figure out why it is in the "To Do" list. Once this initial screening is over, you are left with work that has to be worked upon. Don't be in a hurry to execute all the tasks at once. The week that you are currently in should be set-up to achieve your big goals and work-related deliverables. Small tasks if not urgent can be deferred or managed in one cluster at one go.

STEP 5: CATEGORIZE

The next step is to take the tasks/activities belonging to the above categories is to put them into **rational subgroups or similar work groups**. Work can be collected into various combinations of categories based upon the criteria we use. However, to initiate this discussion we can start with the basic two types of work that we described earlier. These are called **Tasks** and **Projects**.

Tasks are small and very often single action activities which we keep doing throughout the day. Getting up to prepare coffee, calling someone, commuting to work, writing an e-mail, going shopping are all tasks.

Tasks can be further divided into **Personal** and **Job/Business** Tasks and further-on into **Daily** and **General** Tasks. **Daily Tasks** includes activities like grooming, commuting, maintaining expenses, eating etc. General tasks are like infrequent one-time events like making payments, shopping, buying groceries, visiting a doctor or going for a health checkup etc.

Projects similarly can be further divided into **Personal** and **Job/Business**. If a project is something you aspire for and will lead to a significant improvement in your life, then it becomes a **Goal**. Projects themselves can be **Short**, **Medium** and **Long** based upon their magnitude and time required.

The Figure shown below depicts the basic categorization into Tasks and Projects and further into Daily and General Work. The Projects are divided into Long (may take months or even years), Medium (few weeks to a several months) and Short term (few hours to several days) projects.

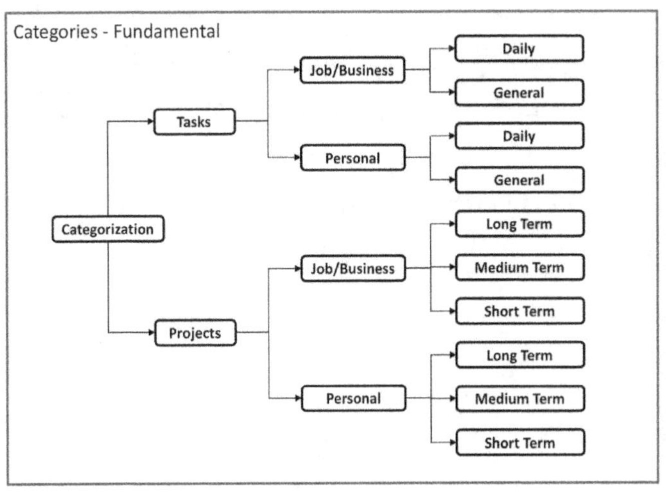

One critical thing that you need to understand is that the projects and tasks have to be executed. It's of no use to create a list of tasks and projects that you don't have the capacity to accomplish. Thus, the main purpose of this step is to chafe out what is vitally important for you and what can be taken up later or dropped altogether.

Let's begin with the next step now that will further allow you to segregate and ultimately prioritize work. Here we organize work into natural categories that act as containers where you can park work. It's like a row of labeled jars on a kitchen shelf. We pick and choose what to cook and mix on a particular day.

The aim will be to however, see that the work we are collecting on the shelf must keep on moving and only a limited amount is taken that we can process per our priority and bio-rhythm. Here is where the actual start of our basic principle of balance starts.

A day requires us to play different roles depending upon whom we are with but broadly it can categorized into Job/Business, Self, Family, and Social. Then there are various categories which cut across categories like finance, health, recreation etc.

Categorization can help prioritize and also make us aware of where our focus should lie. It also helps to visualize the work distribution in terms of the various roles we have to play in our daily life.

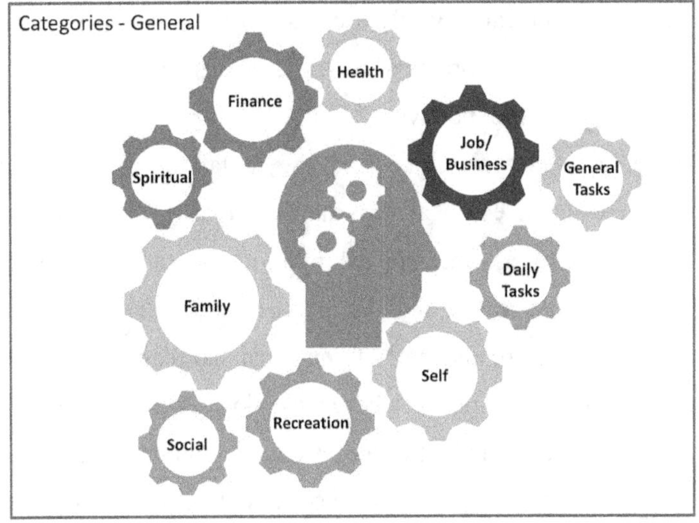

A preponderance of tasks/projects related to a single role is a sign of imbalance and possible stress in that area. These categories can further be subdivided into more meaningful sub-categories.

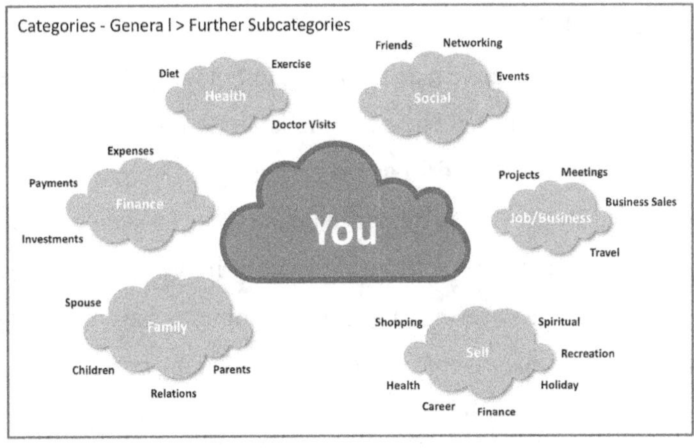

Another categorization is possible in relation to certain contexts. For example, you can have separate lists in relation to your work, family members, car, projects etc. A category helps in putting the work in the right perspective.

Some core categories and what they entail are given below. What you will notice right away is that there is a significant amount of overlap in categories. For example, if you have two called Family and Finance, you will see that the financial needs of your family members are also part of your financial planning process in your Finance category. You have the option to then set-up family finance subcategory under finance or keep it all in one place under Family. Having, too many categories becomes a bit unwieldy, therefore keep your categories based on what you can manage.

Greater is your effort to make money, greater would be the amount of work coming from the roles which require you to be more active in your public space.

WORK-RELATED

Millions of people are engaged in various types of jobs in offices, restaurants, shops, etc. Their routine is pretty predictable being caught in a nine to five drill day in and day out. They spend their nine to five routine driven by someone else. They hand over control over their time to others. Money and Security are what they get in return. On the other hand, we have people owning their own businesses like manufacturing, selling or providing services. Their time can also be equally fragmented to manage various aspects of their business. In business, unlike jobs, there is no clear separation of duties and demarcation between personal and public space as it's left to our discretion. Housewives are a special category of workers who are engaged in managing their homes and family. They are virtually on duty round the clock. Work-related tasks and projects can be classified under various subcategories like specific projects, meetings, finance, sales etc.

SELF

This category encompasses all aspects of your being; health, finance, recreation, professional, educational etc. Before we can manage our family or career or business, we need to manage ourselves. Lack of attention to self leads to diminishing capabilities in other areas of our life.

At the same time spending too much time in this category is an indication that you are neglecting other important categories like your family or spending little time for social interactions.

FAMILY

We are tied intrinsically to our families. Beginning with parents and siblings when we are unmarried, to our spouse and then children, we keep expanding our families and also keep adding social circles. Tasks and Projects may emanate from our family obligations. These can include small tasks providing for daily sustenance to big projects like for e.g. buying a new house or marriage of children . The list of tasks and projects which can come out of this category are significant for us and requires careful planning as they can be pretty urgent and can conflict with our job/ business schedules.

SOCIAL

This category is related to our existence as a social animal. We need each other not only for supporting/helping in our job/business pursuits but also to meet our recreation and emotional needs. Our friends, relations, business associates, colleagues all fall under this category. Spending time socially is a great stress-buster as meeting other people leads to exchange of ideas, and also promotes further cooperation in many other areas including work.

FINANCE

This category is a huge black hole that doesn't devour your time but it will keep you stressed day in and day until you get a handle on your financial levers. The levers essentially are expenses management, budgeting and investing. Managing money is one of the key skills and habit that you will have to inculcate to be able to support your family properly, plan for the future, save and have the disposable income to buy things of luxury or be able to plan recreation time at restaurants, hotels, resorts, and other entertainment avenues.

HEALTH

You live inside your body. Health is the most important area of our life. It consists of activities like exercising, reactive or proactive doctor visits. Physical fitness is of paramount importance if you have to master your day. Improved planning and productivity will come to naught if the energy is lacking to execute. Health should be one of your priority categories by default. Nothing should come above health.

Further categorization of these categories is also possible to further define important work categories as shown below.

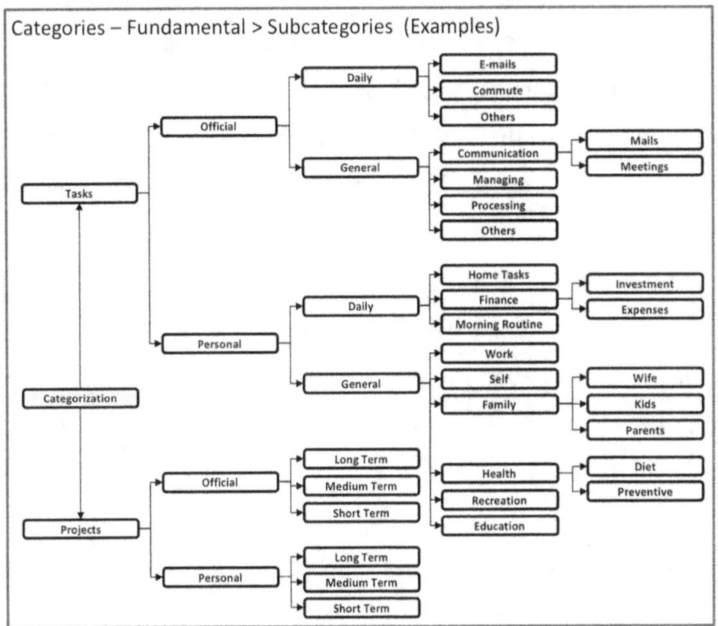

ALIGNMENT TO GOALS

One final category, but perhaps the most important one that you have to create is that for your goals. Goals are an attempt at putting your dreams on paper in the form of a plan or project. Goals are a special category of projects which very often are not urgent or even seem important, but they are key projects which takes your life forward and gives it purpose. Goals, when combined with passion and talent, can take you to great heights.

If ever you want to do a thing that consumes you, you will only do that thing without any consideration. However, most of the work in everyday life is not that interesting or consuming. In the everyday business of life to move forward or to reach somewhere, the journey is usually dour and tardy but it has to be gone through to reach the promised land of your dreams and aspirations. It is that one single focus that will root your existence into something meaningful. Find that one thing that will fuel you for a lifetime. Ignore this, and you may delve in mediocrity and monotony forever.

A typical day should ideally be spent pursuing your most important goals. But life is not that simple. On a typical day, you would find being pulled by multiple priorities. If you are employed then it becomes even more difficult. The starting potential can become prohibitive for personal tasks and projects. *But the Goals are what make our life worth living*. Even when a good part of a day or a week is spent making your living, make it a point to create this category and plan it into your day in whatever small measure it is possible.

There is something magical about goal setting. Define a goal and immediately you feel charged. Now start tuning the goal more accurately. Does it seem measurable, realistic? Add a timeline and you have a worthwhile target to pursue. Wait! Does it make your heart jump and you want to begin immediately, otherwise revisit your goal and add elements which you feel passionately for and are motivated to achieve quickly. Goals can be short-term, mid-term and long-term. Goals must be Specific, Measurable, Achievable, Realistic and Time-bound`.

You can set goals for all important areas of your life. There are no restrictions on the number of goals you can set for yourself but in terms of how much you can handle, start with a smaller number of goals.

Here is a general methodology to help set goals quickly using principles of vivid visualization.

STEP 1: GET INTO A SERENE STATE

For visualization to work well you need to reach a calm and composed state devoid of any distractions. It will take some time to be into that state.

STEP 2: WRITING THE KEY OBJECTIVES

Clearly think of / write down what you want to achieve from the visualization as your mind can take you or make you assume any persona that you can imagine.

STEP 3: WRITE DOWN YOUR VISUALIZATION

Yes, it works. Essentially you are trying to create a story in your mind. If the story is already laid out, you can focus on the other aspects of visualization like making it more vivid. Visualization is a story of which you are the scriptwriter, director and actor all rolled into one. Make your story as graphic as possible so that it looks more and more realistic and make it big, colorful and logical. Visualization is a call for action, an important trigger that will keep you on track in your journey towards your goal. To begin with, have a story to last anything between 5 -10 minutes. Stress on the key parts of the script and words that you would like to stress upon.

STEP 4: MAKE YOUR VISUALIZATION VIVID

Add colors, sounds and action to make it larger than life. The next thing to do is to take some time to make an image of your goal in your mind, make it specific, make your image clear, make it bright, make it big, make it a moving image (if you want to), make it wide-screen and make it really colorful. Next, add sound, make it loud, hear the sounds around you, hear what you are saying to yourself and what other people are saying to you. Now all that remains is to add into your vision what feelings you are experiencing and try to display these feelings in your own body language and posture as if you had achieved this goal right now. See the changes that come to your life after you have achieved your goal.

Write down in a diary or at an accessible place what you have visualized. Replay it often and always see yourself achieving your goal in the end. You will soon become motivated and start believing in the possibility that the goal can actually fructify in your life.

5.3 CHOICE

The choice is our prerogative and we exercise it every moment of our life without even realizing it. From when to wake-up, exercise, selecting clothes, making decisions, choosing what to focus on are some of the hundreds of choices we make every day. Is it a surprise that our choices determine what we achieve and become?

Life gives us many choices every day and we are spoilt for choice. We flit around doing one thing or the other .Then we leave and move on to our next thing that catches our fancy. The monkey mind never rests. Nothing seems important or worthy enough to give our full attention it deserves. Our daily routine makes us forget our lack of purpose. This pattern goes on repeating and slowly we wither away perpetually in a zone of "going to act".

Thus choice has to be done carefully and methodically. Once the work has been categorized, we are in a position to exercise our choices and prioritize our work.

There is always a tussle between various conflicting tasks at any given moment you are deciding what to do next. It's always a struggle if you have not prioritized and scheduled what needs to be done. Urgent tasks are basically the tasks that demand our immediate attention normally having associated deadlines and when we forget or have not decided upon them, they become even more urgent.

Important activities are about self-growth and are really the ones in which our real happiness lies. But in our daily disorganized lives, we keep them at bay waiting for some mythical opportune time. The reason you are reading this book is proof that you want to act on what's important.

Life is all about priorities and your day should be spent executing around your priorities and not around managing noise. Once you are able to do this your daily struggles with managing time would be over.

Whatever may be your situation from being a housewife to a CEO of a company, the fact remains that you can lead a better life by simply managing around your priorities and finding ways of controlling noise. The demands of the day are complex, dynamic, and there are no formal schools or training that we receive to manage our day.

Our goal should be never to neglect "Important" category tasks at the expense of "Urgent" category which demands immediate attention and is deadline-driven. A medical emergency is one exception to the above two categories as it is both important and urgent.

If we can overcome our inclination and programming to respond instinctively to "Urgent" tasks and plan them so as to even anticipate them, we can then wrap the "Urgent" around the "Important" and make sure that each one of them gets their due place during the course of the day. Urgent tasks come in all shapes and sizes, some puny and some of monstrous proportions. They all need to be dealt with separately based upon their complexity.

"Urgent" tasks by themselves are also important as not doing them have repercussions. However, if they are linked to your goals, vision and mission, then they are important as they are helping you in fulfilling your goal. In the absence of "Urgent" and inaction on "Important", we slip into a zone of wasting time on tasks which are "Neither Urgent, Nor Important" like watching TV or spending time endlessly on leisure activities.

PRIORITIZATION

Life is just about priorities but we hardly give it a thought. Lack of priority combined with unbridled choice causes havoc with our time and makes us indulge in trivia or just waste time in managing noise. Prioritization is the act of choosing tasks and projects which can make a big difference to your life. If we can ruthlessly prioritize what is good for us, then life turns into a series of fulfillments which otherwise would remain in the realms of fantasy.

PRIORITIZATION APPROACHES

There are various ways to prioritize, some people instinctively know how to act on what is important. Lesser mortals are plain frozen by the prospect of having to work on something which troubles them or makes them face the unknown.

We will do the prioritization at two levels.

LEVEL 1: BASED ON IMMEDIACY - IMPORTANCE

One of the best frameworks to follow is the Eisenhower approach of clubbing tasks between Urgent and Important and combinations thereof. The "Eisenhower Method" is credited to Dwight D. Eisenhower, the 34th President of USA who famously once said that "I have two kinds of problems, the urgent and the important. The urgent are not important, and the important are never urgent".

The following approach adopts the principle but makes it simpler.

Type A: Essential: Immediate – Important

The Immediate and Important are the tasks which can't wait howsoever the time they may take like a client meeting, catching a flight, a medical emergency etc.

Type B: Life-Changing: Not Immediate – Important

This is the main category the tasks and projects within which will take your life forward

Type C: Noise: Immediate – Not Important

This category has been described earlier in Chapter 3. Noise if not controlled engulfs your day. And moves up to Type A: Immediate - Important: Essential Category. It is thus important to isolate noise and keep it confined to Type C: Noise category only.

Type D: Waste: Not Immediate – Not Important

This is the category which we tend to fall into in the absence of anything urgent and important.

Given below are examples of activities in the form a matrix divided into a four blocker diagram. The combination of Immediate and Important gives us the categories listed above.

Prioritization Matrix

	Immediate	Not Immediate
Important	**Type A : Essential** • Requires immediate attention • Last minute activities, deadline driven	**Type B : Life Changing / Enriching** • Progress related / Makes Life Better • Act on Big Goals / Priorities • Planning- Family/Health/Financial / Self-Development • Rejuvenation-Recreation
Not Important	**Type C : Noise** • Follow-ups • Small Tasks • Travelling • Payments / Shopping • Looking for things	**Type D : Waste** • Chatting • Online Browsing • Social Media • Other Non Value added activities

LEVEL 2: BASED ON RESTRICTING OUR CHOICE TO A CHOSEN FEW

Almost 100 years ago, the President of the Bethlehem Steel company in the USA was Charles M Schwab. His company was struggling with inefficiency and Schwab didn't know how to improve it, so he called in Ivy Lee, a well-known efficiency expert at the time. This was his prescription to his company's executives which proved to be hugely successful and is recommended by productivity experts even today.

THE IVY LEE METHOD

- Draw up a list of the six most important work that has to be achieved the next day. Do this a day earlier when creating the Master of the Day schedule.
- Prioritize the work items in the order of their importance. You can choose from the top categories and can be a mix of immediate tasks/threads and important ones.
- The next day, to begin with, only focus on the first task. Complete it till moving onto the next one. Keep at it till you are done for the day. Any unfinished tasks need to be added to the Super Six list for the next day. In case of a project, even if you can finish the project thread scheduled for the day, it's enough. You have made progress.

This method basically is about limiting the choices so as not to overwhelm us with a list of unending tasks and projects. There is nothing sacrosanct about doing six tasks. It could be five or four depending upon the complexity and time required. If a complex task is urgent and of high value, it will envelop your entire day and you may forget everything else.

These approaches can be used in conjunction with each other. While approach 1 can help identify immediate, not immediate, important and unimportant work the Ivy Lee method can further prune down the choice to just half a dozen important tasks and project threads which can constitutes the work-in-progress making your schedule much more realistic and easy to handle.

METHODOLOGY

1. **Review** all the work listed in various work categories starting with the more important categories like Family, Health, Money and pick the tasks from them.
2. **Pick the tasks and project threads** from your work baskets and the running projects / goals.
3. **Prioritize** your work based upon the prioritization matrix and skim out further the top tasks and threads you would like to line-up during the day.
4. **Separate Noise from the *Immediate* category**. What is left then constitutes a set of priority tasks/project threads, which if not done will have consequences or will delay the achievement of your projects/goals.

EASY TIPS

1) Pareto Living: Pareto principle is one of the most fundamental and beautiful concept also popularly called as the 80:20 rule. It basically states that 80% of the effects comes from 20% of the causes or, to put it another way we can say "It states that 80% of your results come from 20% of your efforts". The implications that it has for our life is huge. It basically cuts down your work by 80% in anything that you may be trying to achieve. So if you are preparing for an examination, it does not mean that 80% of the paper would come from 20% of the syllabus, rather it means that 80% of your outcomes will come from 20% of the preparation actions. Thus, choose the key actions that will bring you the results faster and commit to getting those activities done on priority.

5.4 DECISION

Lack of a decision is sometimes the underlying reason for our inaction. Our life is choked by a lack of decisions. That's why we have to be pushed to make a decision. This is the time to question your inclination to undergo the task or a project. One of the key skills you have to keep practicing is to take decisions. It is highly recommended that you don't proceed with execution without taking a decision. Just like you have to exercise your arms, legs, and abs to develop these areas, you have to exercise your decision muscles.

Here is a general methodology to help you decide quickly and firmly.

METHODOLOGY

- **Identify the Options you have:** This is a fairly simple step as it involves listing the options you have. It's very important here to visualize the end outcome in as much detail as possible to etch the picture or movie in your mind. Spend a good amount of time in creating that movie. Make it so enjoyable that you want to see it again and again.

- **Create Criteria based on factors that are important for you.** This is a critical step. It will bring-out on what you want the outcome to be. For example, in case you have a job offer, then if you have already set a criterion that you will consider future growth prospects over a higher salary, then the decision becomes much easier.

- **Apply the Criteria to each of the choices:** The next step is about applying the criteria to choices you have identified in step 1. You will find none of the choices will completely fit your criteria. This is how life is. It is full of compromises. But still, a decision has to be made.

- **Take the Decision and never repent it ever:** This is the moment of reckoning as the decision is finalized and is ready to be executed. Resolve never to repent any decision that you make. The more you beat yourself on making a wrong decision, the more likely you are to hesitate taking your very next decision.

- **See it through:** As soon as we make a decision we are engulfed by anxiety about whether we have taken the right decision or not. This is natural and healthy as it allows you to keep vigil and see through your decision. However, please understand that there are no right or wrong decisions, you only are choosing a course which will bring different results.

EASY TIPS

▶ **Simply Decide:** The main decision, before you actually come down to making everyday decisions is that, do you want to lead a more orderly and fulfilling life? Do you want to reach somewhere where your dreams reside or you simply want to simply continue a repetitive and predictive journey? This is an overarching fundamental decision which you will have to take. If you are fully convinced on this one, you are more likely to take more bold decisions.

▶ **Think:** This word says it all and at first glance, you might say that this is what you do all the time. But the fact is that what we do is actually shallow thinking most of the time. We only respond and use all our thinking skills to only work-related matter and hardly a deep thought to our other aspects of life like our family, health and self-reflection. The MOD framework forces you to think and act deeply in all the important areas of your life. Develop the skill to step back and reflect upon the "Vital Four" as you set goals and take decisions for each one of them.

Again, this is obvious but you would be surprised to see how much we are slaves to our daily habits and thought patterns. Just pick up what you did last week and you will see a familiar daily pattern emerging. This same pattern repeats and converts into months and years. Thinking can help analyze and breaking these patterns but we hardly consciously make time to just think. If those fears or way of approaching problems and behaviours are not re-thought, you would keep on repeating the same old tired mind scripts and keep getting the same results.

In 1772, Franklin wrote a letter to one of his friends and described the first account of a Pros & Cons list to aid balanced and objective decision making. This is what he proposes.

"To begin with take a sheet of paper with a vertical line dividing the page into two longitudinal sections over a period of a few days.

He calls for listing all the Pros and Cons of a situation as all the reasons / motives might not strike our mind all at once. All the possible reasons are listed their relative importance is compared and the ones having equal importance are struck out. If more than one reason is equal to one reason on either side, then even multiple reasons can be struck out on either side. If two reasons are equal to three on both sides, cross out all five. Though the weights can't be precise but as a mathematical quantity, they still aid decision making as per Franklin. He says, that it helps him in not taking a hasty decision and also understand the drawbacks of what he is about to enter.

The pros and Cons method works well in helping us in listing the major factors that should be considered in making the decision. If we add weights to the factors we can further clarify what value we give to a particular factor. In the end, we are much better off and feel more at ease in making a decision compared to just shooting in the dark or just going with our gut feeling.

5.5 CLARIFY

Once the decision is taken, we got to seek clarity about the work to be done. To get clarity quickly take help of someone who has done it before or an expert. In case you have a team, the work gets done more quickly. Clarity will lead you to your goal even before you get started. It's like the visual achievement of the goal.

The basic questions that you have to ask for getting clarity are the following:

- What am I trying to achieve?
- What do I need to get started?
- Who can help me?
- By when do I want to finish it?
- Will this make me achieve anything out of the Big Four goals of my day i.e. Healthier, Happier, Better and Richer?

Here is a general methodology to help clarify the purpose and steps of the work you are about to undertake.

METHODOLOGY

- **Start from Basics** and try to understand the start and the endpoint. Begin with the final outcome in mind and trace your way backward.
- **Understand the Boundaries:** Understand where the end point is. Sometimes we go beyond what is required to be done.
- **Visualise:** Visualize the task and activities in as much detail as possible & see yourself executing and getting into a climax before finishing the work.
- **Create Project Threads:** In case of a Project, write down the "threads" (refer Chapter 3) involved in the form of a plan; activity, duration, and deadline. Threads are value added activities geared for action in being specific and progressive i.e. they must lead us to the next thread. Understand the magnitude, the difficulty involved and the support required and revise the plan if needed. A thread must begin when the preceding thread terminates and they lead to incrementally

completing the project. Every thread completed should take you a step closer to completion.

EASY TIPS

- **Begin with the End in Mind:** Sometimes your mind has to see it before it believes it and before you can actually figure out how can be done. Take a notebook and pen to create your thoughts on paper starting from the end. Completely THINK over it and write down your steps and thoughts on paper.

- **Start from First Principles:** I somehow always come back to this principle after breaking my head trying to do multiple things. "First Principles" basically means starting from scratch from the first building block. As you do that a sort of organisation happens in your head and your brain is able to visualise the task much better. Think simple and then gradually build it and you will invariably get the focus and creativity that you desire every single time.

- **Keep it Simple to Begin With:** Your first effort in starting a new task should be to get a head start and grasp. If you have to think of Top 3 tasks to be begin with, then what would that be? Just focus on that and take them to completion. Some Tasks tend to be long winded. Don't think perfection here. Just create a "minimum acceptable workable draft" which is good to be "shipped" or used. Start using the method, solution or approach you have developed so you can test the hypothesis and gradually building upon it and taking it to the next level. Sometimes in all our zeal to create something unique we get bogged down in details. Knowledge if not applied and monetised is worthless.

- **Eat the Elephant:** If ever I have to tell you one single trick that can potentially change your life, then this is the one that you will read in the next few lines. Ignore this and you suffer. Generalising and clustering afflict every mind. Stop looking at work as a homogenous whole. If we do that, we immediately sow seeds of procrastination. Our mind does not like lack of clarity or something that doesn't seem achievable. Smaller tasks are much more convincing to us as they seem doable and keep moving us forward and when we see we tend to see failure as our inability to achieve a goal or considering work as too much effort and not even starting. There is a beauty about completion. However, the prognosis of the failure may lie with one very basic concept of achievement that is metaphorically called as "Eat the Elephant". In simple terms, it means to breakdown a seemingly huge task or a goal into small manageable parts and subparts and then slowly nibbling away at those parts, till you have finished it. You can accelerate the process by involving more people, by delegation or deciding not to eat a portion at all. This principle applies to our thinking also wherein we paint an entire situation as good or bad depending upon our emotional state while if we try to break down the issue into what went right and what went wrong, we will be perhaps much better off. Trying to *eat the elephant* in one whole gulp is an exercise in delusion and perpetual frustration.

- **Ask for Help:** This is one act that can exponentially accelerate your efforts and dramatically raise your productivity. The people around you are great accelerators. If I look back at what I have achieved over the years, one common factor has stood out. It wasn't achieved without the help of others. Maybe, it was that small piece of information you wanted from your colleague to achieve a breakthrough in your project or that reference you got from a friend to meet someone who could help. It could be your team who could be working extra hard, so you can shine in your organisation and not the least, it could be your wife, who tirelessly works in the background to see all your daily needs are met and you can focus on your work. We are constantly being helped one way or the other, if we are working in isolation, then we are being our own biggest bottleneck.

- **Create a Deadline:** Deadlines are magical. Without a deadline the intent is not clear, nor are you primed to finish a task at hand. More hours doesn't mean more work. Our mind is like an untapped goldmine. It has all the reserves to help you fulfill your dreams. It works as fast or as slow as you want it to. You are controlling it all the time. However, in case of a deadline this control is taken over by an external factor that pulls us with a force that intensifies based upon its outcome and how much time remains. External deadlines will work even better. Use deadlines and witness the magic that happens in you and what you are trying to achieve. They make you come alive and propel action. Keep a deadline for tasks which don't seem to have an immediate one. Deadlines can also be fixed at sub-tasks level or at the overall task and project level.

- **Value:** When creating threads you can also use the Value criteria. Check whether the thread is specific enough to be executed and will add significant value to your project or goal.

- **Link to your passion:** Link the work to what is your passion spot. You may have a passion for gadgets, cars, music or whatever else it might be. However, in the name of earning a living you may be miles off your passion. Don't fret, there is still hope. The only thing which is stopping you from going for your passion is you. It might be a bit too late and you don't have the time for it. However, even a small act in the realm of your passion will fill you with new energy. Who knows, maybe this small step may turn into a series of steps soon and before you know, your passion is alive and kicking. In the end, who made the change? You did!

- **Self-Knowledge:** We are a power created out of the infinite universe. The fact you are born in human form and have a life to live is reason enough to believe that you are empowered. It's only your upbringing and other environmental factors that may have induced pessimism and lack of self-belief.

5.6 ORGANIZE

Organization is linked to Changeover and Set-up time we read earlier. Set-up time can increase drastically if things are not organized. Disorganization mixes with lack of clarity to raise the starting potential. Any work that you will take up will need a few accessories, some phone number, your laptop, pen and paper and anything else. It is imperative that you must have them in near sight or soon the very act of finding them can increase the starting potential immeasurably. At the same time, the task gets lost somewhere under the heaps of noise that is lingering all around us. Very soon, the benefits, deadlines associated with the task get forgotten.

The organization is the first step towards perfection. Without organization, you won't even get started. So, let's get organized.

Some basic rules of organization are spelt out in a marvelous Japanese quality practice of 5S which has been used in manufacturing facilities and even in offices. However, the principles are applicable in our personal life at home also. 5S in Japanese stands for:

Sort (Seiri) Separate between necessary and unnecessary things and getting rid of what you do not need.

Set in order (Seiton) This is the practice of orderly storage so the right item can be picked efficiently (without waste) at the right time, easy to access for everyone. A place for everything and everything in its place.

Shine/Sweeping (Seiso) This step entails keeping your workplace, computer, tools, and documents clean and tidy.

Standardize (Seiketsu) This basically means to create rules and standards for maintaining the gains from steps 1,2,3 above.

Sustain (Shitsuke) This involves inculcating the habit to maintain the standards in step 4 above to maintain the gains from steps 1,2,3.

How can this quality technique help us in organizing and managing our daily life better? Let's understand how we can apply this methodology to organize our daily routine and the stuff that we use.

Here is a general methodology based on the 5S method described above, to get you started on the path to organization.

METHODOLOGY

- Applying the principle of *Sort (Seiri)*, separate the necessary from the unnecessary. Throw away items that you have not used for a long time. Chances are you won't need them at all. Store all the documents, stationery, files and other stuff that you use daily or frequently near your place of work, so you won't have to search for them. Remove all clutter around your workspace and organize all your projects into neat files. Label all the stuff around you so that you don't have to think again about the reason why a box is there or a file exists.
- Use *Set in order (Seiton)* to help organize things that you

need around you which you use most often. The habit of keeping things back to the place where you picked it from will pay handsome dividends and will prevent frustration.

- Use *Shine/Sweeping (Seiso)* to keep your workplace and tools (laptop, stationery, files, documents) in prime condition as this is critical to your productivity.
- Use *Standardize (Seiketsu)* to lay down the rules for organization, say on your laptop, paper files, drawers, cabinets etc.
- Use *Sustain (Shitsuke)* to organize your workplace and tools as a matter of habit.
- Use these steps to organize all the stuff, documents, your daily gadgets like laptop, mobile phone, tablets and whatever else you might be using. Organization will lead to a serene state wherein you will feel as if a load has been taken off your head. The noise surrounding everyday activities like searching for stuff, keeping loads of unnecessary stuff which perhaps you will never use and the inability to get started will reduce significantly.

5.7 SCHEDULE

For becoming the Master of the Day, you must claim the day and own every second of it. An unscheduled day is an open invitation for anything that catches your fancy, inaction, people claiming it for their purpose and many other wastes that we have been discussing. Scheduling is about diarizing your tasks or threads and choosing a time slot to perform them based upon the effort required. The schedule is one of the key habits that you have to learn to get started. A task or project thread scheduled will have a high probability of getting done sooner or later if it has been scheduled. Planning activities within the day forces you to think of the size of the job at hand, your capacity to deal with it, delegation or help required, organization required etc. In short, it forces you to plan for action and add value. So, this is where the rubber meets the road. You have placed your car on the track and you are ready to race at a pre-decided time.

Pick prioritized tasks/project threads and schedule them depending upon your productivity curve. If the task requires you to do creative thinking, choose a time when your mind is fresh.

Scheduling a task requires you to consider the following:

▶ **Time & Effort Required:** If a task or project thread takes a long time and involves significant effort than what you have right now, then you have to either thread it further or you have to schedule it for a later time. In any case, while scheduling you will have to take a cluster of days like a week or a month to spread the threads.

▶ **Energy:** Your energy curve during the day fluctuates and you know best when you are in your most productive zone. For most of us, morning is the best time to focus on complex tasks and projects if nothing else is scheduled. Thus, keeping a habit of utilizing your golden hours will change your life completely.

▶ **Deadline:** If the task is important and the deadline is looming then, you have few options other than to schedule the task at the expense of other tasks and even when your batteries are down.

SCHEDULING APPROACHES

Schedule the tasks/project threads at preferably 30 minutes intervals to begin with. You can go down further to 15 minutes if you can handle it. However, there is a more radical approach made popular by the likes of Bill Gates and Elon Musk of planning your time at an interval of 5 minutes.

While I will not also prescribe 5-minute planning, to begin with, but it is a great way to become cognizant of how time slips away in small intervals of time. This approach might be overkill at the beginning but at a day level but you can earmark one hour per day to start with where you can cluster all your noise; Small tasks (payments, organizing, short calls, nags and other miscellaneous tasks which won't take more than 5 minutes). This will give you the flavor of what 5 min planning is all about. You will notice that it also resonates with the concept of threads and "Value Addition" I introduced earlier.

As you become more organized and matured in the methodology, you can start experimenting with adding more such hours having 5-minute intervals.

I am presently on the 5-minute interval schedule and my observations are as under:

- Sensitivity to time slipping by 5 minutes a time becomes much acute.

- Productivity increases as our inclination to become distracted reduces.

- I have one hour each day which I call as the "Power Hour" where I cluster all the less than 5-minute tasks and start executing them ruthlessly. It doesn't matter if it takes more than 5 minutes, However, if I am getting stuck or getting delayed, then I move on to the next task and try to get back to it later. Consider it to be a game. You have say 12 tasks to do. How many do you end up with? More you do better your score is!

- I need to manage for having a way to carry a schedule that shows me my activities at 5-minute intervals. I personally am managing by creating an excel sheet which I find to be infinitely malleable but I won't recommend this as the means to manage if you find this cumbersome.

- I was always struggling to create a log of the activities that I had done for analysis, but now I have a record which I can analyze at the end of the week.

- It keeps my tendency to multi-task under check as I can analyze those "flip-overs" during the day and I am always surprised at the number of change-overs self-created or externally triggered.

WEEKLY / MONTHLY PLANS

A week or a month are aggregated day clusters and their planning is very important if you have to keep your MOD plan intact. Project threads, in any case, will take weeks or months before they are wrapped-up. Managing weekly / monthly schedules gives you near term perspective to distribute work more evenly and factor days when your schedule is already chockablock. This is called as load leveling. It also helps avoid getting taken by surprises. A week provides the nearest horizon in which your days will come packaged. It is very important to see your weekly schedule along with your daily schedule to see how your key tasks and projects/ goals will progress. Everyone in any profession has at least one day in the week when there is a holiday while a five day week in corporates is the norm. This means that we can act as "unemployed" during these two days. Your schedule for these two days will be different from your normal week day. Similar is the case for other holidays as well. Thus, many of the review tasks, personal goals pursuits can only be done on these days.

It is also important to review these goals at the end of the week to measure your progress. Similarly, a monthly schedule will show how your month is lined up, the noise in the way and the important planned, unplanned tasks and events which if not visualized can potentially de-rail your MOD plans. It is surprising that how less we refer to our monthly plans as they are an invaluable "Bird Eye" view of what lies ahead in the coming weeks. Master of the Day planning keeps the weekly and monthly horizons well within view to let nothing come in the way of your goal achievement. Weekly and monthly View templates are provided in the Annexure. A personal planner diary is a simple and efficient tool. It records your day events and also provides weekly, monthly and yearly views. However, it is up to you as to in which form you would like to maintain it. Alternatively, you can also maintain it on your smartphone or in a pull-out file.

Here is a general methodology to schedule what is important for you.

METHODOLOGY

1. Choose high priority task or a project thread and schedule them in the Zone of Productivity

2. Assign the time slots depending upon the effort required, deadline and your energy levels. Bring the prioritized top tasks and project threads for the day and assign them. Your day will already have fixed slots for your Fixed Personal & Job / Business Tasks. Apart from that there would be other job/ business related activities like meetings etc.

3. Schedule a Power Hour with 5 minute interval to tackle your noise and other tasks which should on an average take less than 5 minutes.

4. Once scheduled, execute and make adjustments if the task or project thread overspills or you run into an unanticipated road-block.

EASY TIPS

▶ **Be tough with yourself:** Start now by doing something today that you have been putting off. It may be a small or a large matter. Sometimes all it takes to discipline the child within us is to do the thing that we are deciding to put off. Just hold your hand during that moment of weakness and drag yourself into doing it.

▶ **Plan, Plan, Plan:** This seems like a recipe to over-process things, but I can't stress more on the importance of planning in our normal day to day existence in a big city, and life seeped in complexities, planning your day, week, month will keep you floating like a butterfly cut down the surprises, improve your productivity manifold and add immeasurable happiness in your life. Remember if you are not planned, then even without realizing you will waste time, all the time. With no sense of time during the day, activities and idle time will just stretch more than necessary. An e-mail or a phone will take longer, conversations might go on and on, a particular activity might just engulf your day.

▶ **Eat the Frog:** The famous American writer and humourist, Mark Twain once quipped that "If it's your job to eat a frog, it's best to do it first thing in the morning. And if it's your job to eat two frogs, it's best to eat the biggest one first." This says it all. One of the simplest ways to apply this approach is to get up and force yourself to do the job you have been avoiding for so long. Sometimes one small task can reduce stress exponentially spread over many pending big tasks. This trick also breaks the dreaded starting potential. We may not realize it but many critical tasks which we loathe or which raise our anxiety levels hinder our productivity as we are constantly living under the shadow of having to do that work sooner or later and the anxiety keeps rising.

▶ **Fixed time working:** This is like making a definite time slot of the day booked for a particular activity so much so that come what may you stick to it. Persistence is an incredible thing combined with a habit. Doing the same thing repeatedly brings results like nothing else. Try to fix a time for a productive activity like exercising, writing and soon you will see the results.

We have already seen that in the first two verticals of the E-Framework i.e. Selection and Understanding, how we handle incoming work and make it ready for processing. In the next chapter, we will look at the next two verticals of the E-Framework i.e. Execution and Completion which has three elements each.

E-Framework – Execution & Completion

6.1 INTRODUCTION

Execution and Completion are the next two verticals of the E-Framework having three elements each. You need to be battle ready to take work lined up, focus on it intensely and have the most optimal approach to take it forward. Work can be achieved in many ways, slow or fast, simple or bloated. Once, the work has started it is easy to let go of it at the next distraction or due to any other valid reasons. However, completion is the logical conclusion for any work and further, it can be further evolved to make it even better and useful.

6.2 STATE

Achieving the "state" means warming yourself up to prepare for action. It's a physical and mental trigger to prepare for action. We look at work from a "Cold" State and from there most of our doubts arise. A cold state is an off-work state when mentally we are disengaged to take up anything significant. In normal time, we are relaxed and directionless. If things are normal we take it easy. If people around us are nice we relax even more. There is nothing that really needs our urgent attention. To be in an achievement state is well-nigh very difficult. There is no reason for us to be doing anything that requires us to be alert and compelled to work.

Give up the mortal fears borne out of insecurity and hold your nerves, the last man standing is the winner, not the one who in a mad rush of blood got slain. When you are in the midst of doing something time driven, how is everything happening smoothly? That is because you are in the "State" and primed to "Close". If you do anything else in-between, it will also sail through. If the occasion is big, then it might be the adrenalin rush that is required to get you battle-ready. There are tales galore of the valour of ordinary people who were pushed by circumstances into doing heroic acts which they would have never imagined.

Sometimes the right attire ensures that you reach your state to perform that activity quickly.

I found it very difficult to wake up in the morning during golden hours and once I got up, it was really a challenge to drag myself to look for my jogging suit, shoes, groom and go out for jogging. To overcome this, I realized that if I have the costume ready and have it right next to me on waking up, the starting potential reduced and my mental "state" immediately changed to one of "action". I also made it a point to get out of my home immediately after dressing up and run as per the daily target. I have an incremental goal to be able to run a little more every day. Thus, I have a target to achieve every morning and a mechanism to get into the desired state. Needless, to say this activity has become a habit. Come what may I don't break it!

Compare your level of alertness on a working day vis a vis that on a weekend. Just try concentrating on a weekend on some official or stressful task and see what happens. Most likely we will leave that before long or keep dragging it. To think of giving that all-important client presentation on a weekend in your pajamas seems daunting. But once in your business suit and soaking in the environment of the meeting, you are all geared to deliver and perform. The bottom line is that nothing worthwhile gets done in a pajama suit.

Here is a general methodology to get you started:

METHODOLOGY

1. **Get into the Gear:** As described above getting into the right attire suited to the work you are about to begin puts you into the desired state. You can also achieve the state through meditation or through mindfulness activities.

2. **Clarify the Purpose:** Not just getting into the gear will motivate. You must have a clear purpose and goal for doing the work. The motivation will also come from there.

6.3 FOCUS

In a camera, there is a feature of background blur to sharpen and make the object we are focusing on to stand out. Same way when we focus, all other tasks and thoughts become a blur and that you focus on the subject. When we focus our mind also becomes a camera only focusing on the subject at hand. The MOD approach treats focus as an extension of the state wherein we get focused on the task at hand and get the tasks/project threads loaded into your mind in the morning. This coupled with attaining the "State" in the previous step revs up your mind. It makes your mind unwa-veringly glued to the task at hand. It's actually a culmination of the factors we have discussed earlier viz. clarity, organization, scheduling and state.

METHODOLOGY

1. **Have the Threads Buzzing:** Visit the tasks listed in your MOD Plan for the Day. This comes from the planning you did the previous day. Make adjustments / changes (if any). The entire activity could vary from 15-30 minutes based upon the time available with you before you start for work.

2. **Clear** your mind of any distractions/noise that may be present at that moment.

3. **Begin right away:** There is no point in sitting in your battle armour and just be checking chat messages on your phone. Once the above steps have been taken, your next step has to be pure action. If possible, begin the top task of the day right away to get more focused. However, you might have

only a limited time if you have to begin your commute to work. You would notice that the pressure of having a limited time constraint will increase your productivity dramatically. Even if you are able to do the work only partially, it's fine.

4. **Get Started** with your tasks and project threads on reaching your work place lined up keeping the associated deadlines in perspective. Threading will ensure that this principle is not violated. Pick the Project thread at hand and execute as planned. Visualize the end outcome and revise if needed. Think of the task or the project thread you are trying to execute, the end value and the work boundaries. Do not work without a deadline and always keep it in view and never miss it. It's a promise you have to make yourself and not be greedy.

EASY TIPS

▶ **Give it 15 minutes irst:** Your mind needs to be focused till it gets into the job at hand. Chances are if you can continue doing that one task for fifteen minutes, you will continue doing it even after that.

▶ **Power of One:** It is the ability to focus on only one task or project thread and taking it to completion. This principle is already baked into our prioritization approach when we can only do the top tasks/project threads of the day one by one.

6.4 PRODUCTIVITY

While focus will get you started, productivity will enable you to complete the planned tasks of the day. You can't do everything. Work is a mirage, a bottomless hole. It plays tricks on you. With the tools in your hand like paper, computers, smartphones and instant communication across the world, you may feel that you are in control but the real work or steps that will take to complete will happen in real-time and have to be performed by you or you have to make them happen. To strike a balance between planning and smart action in order to ensure that a particular task gets done quickly should be your target so that it's no longer a time bomb ticking away. By the time you reach the start of your work day, you are ready to execute. You are in the state now and focus has started developing and the plan is laid out for you. Work is already set-up. It's time for action! Begin with your scheduled tasks for the day.

Here is a general methodology to get you up the productivity curve.

METHODOLOGY

- **Focus on Value Addition:** Ensure that you execute the "Value Added" tasks or threads only with very little wastes like waiting, rework, and errors. Apart from you have to ensure that the noise category tasks have been eliminated so you can focus on the job at hand without getting distracted and develop an approach which gives maximum productivity.
- **Apply Productivity Strategies** to quickly finish work within your productivity zone and as per your energy curve. Depending upon your work nature, you will have to

evaluate your work methods to identify the wastes, work-set-up requirements, noise and the effectiveness destroyers.

- **Attain the "Flow":** The first and perhaps the most important step is to actually take the first step. If you have achieved the "state" as described in the previous step then put it to use immediately to get into the concentration zone. The concentration zone is when you are in the state of flow and productivity reaches a crescendo. Top athletes regimen consist of teaching them to "hit the state" when top performance is needed. You can do this too, but it will take practice and patience.

- **Ship or execute the task or complete a thread as per plan.** Remember the "Shipping beats Perfection" maxim. Thus add value as much is needed for satisfactorily doing the work, don't over-process or rework. To put it plainly keep it simple and deliver at the earliest. Also, don't carry any work in progress inventory.

EASY TIPS

▶ **Work Briskly:** This is again a mind trick to get more out of you. Working briskly mimics the climax when work is about to finish and there is a mad rush of many things falling into place at the last moment.

▶ **Concentrate:** Concentrate on the task at hand. Normally within 10-15 minutes focus kicks in and takes your mind off the distractions. Resist the thought or inclination to jump to another task or respond to environmental stimuli like someone interrupting, checking your phone for any new messages or even if you suddenly remember something urgent but can be done slightly later. Just note down the work to be done and get back to what you are doing. Force yourself to keep at what you are doing.

▶ **Using a Timer:** Set a timer in your watch or phone for a set duration say 30 minutes. Once the time is started your challenge is to just focus on the task at hand. You are not allowed to consider anything else. We love games or a challenge. Using a timer pits us against a deadline, a game we have to win!

▶ **Take to Completion:** Our mind is like a giant house full of task rooms. If we keep coming in and going out of these rooms without finishing the tasks, soon we will have a lot of open doors calling us in all directions. It's better to get into one door, spend time there, till the work is finished or till we have moved on to the next. There is a beauty about completion which is like a balm and energiser for our brain all rolled into one. Complete the task that you have at hand. If the scope is very big then cut it down to complete some significant portion of it which is complete in all respects.

▶ **Monitor your Time:** Keep very conscious of your time during the day else your plan will be derailed. Time consciousness is one of the biggest skills that we can learn but it is not taught anywhere. Imagine if your pocket full of money is torn and money is dropping coin by coin. Would you allow it? The same thing happens daily when we waste time. Do we feel the same as losing money? That's where the crux lies. Money lost can be earned back but time once lost cannot be created back. It's like a depreciating account. You have been given a fixed amount. You don't even know how much but it is getting depleted second by second.

▶ **Compartmentalise your Time:** A big task when it becomes urgent will consume you. In order to tackle a time consuming and urgent task, you may have to dedicate a sizable portion of your where you can focus on work without any distraction and not feel guilty or rushed that other tasks are pending and waiting for your action. Don't let that happen! Sometimes, even small tasks become so twisted that they may longer than anticipated. Sacrifices in terms of your other scheduled tasks will have to be factored.

▶ **Create Calculated Imbalance:** While balance is important but there are times when you are bringing a major change to your life or coming out of your comfort zone. A calculated imbalance may be a good thing without compromising on essential elements like health, family and finances. Even while walking forward we have to become imbalanced for a fraction of a second but the end result is advancement. It may involve a lot of activity as the work you are doing may be very hectic but that's the point if it would have been so easy you wouldn't have been needed it in the first place.

6.5 SUSTAIN

Stories are legion on how close people were to success when they gave up, not knowing that the destination was right in front of them. Sustenance is one quality that separates winners from losers. The ability to go the entire distance ensures that even half chances get converted into sure shot successes. The methodology is simple; Just keep at it, don't give up!

Here is a general methodology to persist and sustain what is important and life-changing.

METHODOLOGY

- **Keep on Radar:** Even if you run into a road block, or there is a delay, keeping the project visible will go a long way in getting it completed. Your MOD planning and schedule will ensure that no derailment happens.

- **Work out Alternative Strategies:** If the present approaches are not working then think about alternative approaches. Do whatever it takes to complete. Your dream remains a dream until you take it past the door of realization.

- **Keep Visualizing:** Keep visualizing the "end state" to keep yourself motivated.

- **Apply Deadlines:** Deadlines are what keep you on your toes. A deadline is a trigger for our mind to see an end to an activity else there is no fixed stop for activities that are self-generated.

EASY TIPS

▶ **Habituate for 21 Days:** That's the bare minimum experts say that you need to form a habit. The idea is to repeat the same habit or behaviour repeatedly till it gets ingrained in your routine and mind.

▶ **Treat yourself:** This is about delayed gratification. Make a list of things you have a weakness for. It could be as simple as reaching out to your phone and check WhatsApp messages. From here on you set up targets for yourself. For example, you will only check messages if you have finished a particular task or will indulge in your favorite delicacy if you achieve a particular target.

6.6 COMPLETE

There is a magic about completing a task and even more so a project. It is a complete product that has a final value. Incomplete work howsoever well done still has no value if not completed.

Here is a general methodology to help you complete what you started.

METHODOLOGY

- **Reach the Climax:** For completing something, you will have to undergo some or all of the steps that we have discussed under the "E- Framework" approach. However, once the work approaches completion, certain patterns appear. The work gathers pace. It will hog more of your mind and time space and may push out all the other tasks completely. Thus, the work approaches a climax! It's like the end of the movie when all the things that could go wrong would go wrong before, the hero musters all the courage to surmount the odds to emerge victorious.

- **Be ready for a Sacrifice:** Every worthwhile work demands sacrifice. You can even contemplate giving up one of your passions or indulgences till the time the work gets over or simply resolve to get up only once the work is completed and dispatched.

To illustrate the concept of Climax and Sacrifice let's consider the situation below.

We act differently when we are in the middle of action. It's very difficult to think of a challenging situation in the cold state. For example, imagine you have to make an important strategy presentation to the management, on getting their nod for business expansion. Under stress to perform and not to fail we start vibrating at a different frequency. All our faculties are focussing intensely at the present moment. No wonder we come out of the Board room with a sense of accomplishment. Our effort over the past few days, the data churning, discussions on strategy and course of action, getting opinions, preparing the slides and then multiple dry-runs to refine and create the presentation storyline and possible questions are all practiced. There are no distractions and we are in a state to deliver. This is the climax or the final state. There is sacrifice involved in terms of staying long hours at the office and forgoing all other activities official or personal. Invariably activities reach a crescendo a day before the presentation. Things become more and more chaotic as the presentation approaches and continues till the last moment.

EASY TIPS

▶ **Put up an emergency act:** This mind prank fills you with energy and fooling your mind into believing that a deadline is approaching. After some time, you actually start believing it. Another variant of this approach is to take up a small task while another bigger deadline is looming, for example, you might be ready to leave for office or anywhere else. In the time you have left before you leave, try to do take up a task. Chances are you are already in a state and you will finish that task as well.

6.7 EVOLVE

We all know that mankind evolved from apes. What if evolution stopped then and there? Evolution is the hallmark of humanity. We are here only because life on earth evolved over a period of thousands of years. It has been a slow but definite change.

What if the T-model that Ford launched would have been the final word in personal automobiles and we would still be having those boxy car shapes with crude engines powering them? Our mind thinks incrementally. Once a level is achieved we try to improve upon it as more needs arise because of the change. Change thus is a constant and we human beings are also wired the same way. We change, our thoughts change and only after we reach a destination, do we think of another.

Same way every single work that you do can be evolved to

something better. After completion, evolve is what takes you from good to great. It's a law of nature. Evolution is a beacon that will keep taking you forward and keeps you hinged to your *Vital 4*.

Any task completed is itself a cause for celebration. However, to take that work to the next level is the stuff success is made of. Clinching an order is not an end but a beginning. Similarly receiving praise from a client is not definitive. It has to be reproduced again and again. Then, the expectations go up even further. Successful completion if not converted into learning will lead to stagnation.

Here is a general methodology to help you evolve your achievement to the next level.

METHODOLOGY

1. **Re-arrange and Re-organize:** After work is completed, there are still small pieces of mopping up activities that needs to be done. To close them properly is very important as you may need them later for reference or remind you of what was done and what remained. Create a summary of work done, important decisions, commitments and future tasks if any.

2. **Learn the Lessons:** There are lessons learnt every time we finish an important project. If we don't reflect upon them and think of better ways, we kill evolution and are condemned to repeat the same rigmarole the next time around.

3. **Achieve the Next Level:** Finally, keep working on evolving your output to the next level. One good example that we see very frequently is the software in our computer or smartphone

undergoing updates. Each update is an improvement over the previous one. Similarly, if possible keep evolving your work till you reach its potential or it reaches a logical end.

This brings us to the conclusion of all the elements of the E-Framework which we have discussed in fair detail. We have understood what they are, why they are important, and their methodology along with some quick but vital tips to get you started. In the next chapter we will see how the entire MOD plan is executed.

THE EXECUTION

Execution of the Day

"I wasted time, and now doth time waste me"
William Shakespeare

7.1 THE EXECUTION SEQUENCE FOR MASTER OF THE DAY

In this chapter, we come to the actual application of the Day and E- framework that we discussed earlier and apply it to our day. Again this might vary from person to person based upon how you set-up your day and what you execute in it.

The Golden rule however to follow is to get started immediately. Make part of MOD philosophy functional and start picking the concepts and applying them to your daily routine and thinking patterns. Don't try to adopt everything at once. You will gain knowledge and wisdom gradually.

Master of the Day is the new and efficient you. You are now completely in control of your day and doing things more efficiently.

7.1.1 THE EVENING BEFORE – THE CHANGE-OVER

Stop half an hour before the evening changeover and review how you have done and put down your plan for the next day. Creating your MOD Plan for the next day is perhaps the most important thing that you will do before calling your work day off. MOD planning must be done a day before and all decisions must be taken then and there. Understand that this has to become a daily routine in whatever form you may adopt it. If you skip this, you will probably not have the time again to quickly do it because at that time you are in the "State", all dressed and revved up during the day. Also the present actions or the lack thereof of is still fresh in your mind and can be captured then and there.

Again if you think that planning for next day will come just like that, then you are mistaken. You will have to develop a ritual around it and keep a time limit to achieve it.

You should have a complete end to end list of your tasks and projects listed, categorized, prioritized, threaded and ready to be included in your daily schedule for coming day, week, month and so on. If you don't schedule the tasks during the day and don't manage noise, it will become another issue over which your procrastination would begin. Your priorities are now well identified and have specific actions attached to them. With the segmentation of tasks and projects, you can clearly identify what tasks needs to be taken up on an urgent basis and which ones gets under the noise category. You still though have to deal with unexpected interruptions and developments which might take your focus away from what you have planned.

For putting your tasks and project threads your plan for the day can be done by just writing down the tasks on a piece of paper in unstructured form, in a planner diary, creating templates like the one given in the final section of the book, your smartphone or laptop or on a spreadsheet saved on a cloud drive account like Drop Box, G-Drive etc. accessible to you anywhere through your devices. All phones these days have schedulers which give you a host of add-on features like periodic reminders, sync from your laptop to phone and vice versa. Try to utilize the technology to become more productive and carry your plan with you.

Refer to the threads of ongoing projects and pick them for execution. Pick the priority tasks from your work categories. Schedule them based upon their likely duration and your ability to execute. As you prepare the plan for the next day, you will have to refer to your weekly and monthly plans also to see the impact of today's work on them as they are the immediate clusters of days lying in front of you. Weekly, monthly, yearly templates are available in the annexure.

Apart from these, decisions must be in place and the clarity to proceed must be obtained and reflected in a set of sequential threads that could be executed. If the decision is pending, then don't schedule that work. Next morning, if you are planning to execute tasks and project threads that have major decisional elements involved, then it becomes very difficult to do that at a time when action is what is needed. MOD is about pure unadulterated "Value Added" action which only takes a fraction of the time and eliminates all the wastes that bog you down. Your MOD plan must reflect the key tasks and projects for the day and also should have at least one task picked up from each of the "Vital 4" categories.

Schedule the tasks and project threads around the fixed daily tasks and other engagements of the day. The ability to change over quickly after every task or thread will be a key skill you will have to habituate.

Organize the papers, stuff that you have been working on and everything on your computer, papers, work desk or where you were working so as not to waste time the next morning.

Your MOD plan is now ready! Completely switch off the workday memories. You have done enough. Head for home to begin your last phase of the day. This is when you are again entering personal space and look forward to relaxing and spending quality time with family and socially.

7.1.2 THE NEXT MORNING – ZONE OF PREPARATION / REJUVENATION

The next morning wake up in the Golden Hours and go through your planned routine. Waking up in the Golden Hours is perhaps the biggest challenge that you would have to overcome. But, this would be a game changer as it will be the anchor that will allow your day to go through smoothly as per your MOD plan. For this you must hit the bed early the previous night. Whatever may be the lure at that moment, please put it away if you want to practice the

Master of the Day routine. If you want to get ahead in life, these small adjustments and sacrifices will have to be made. Once you start following the routine, you will find that you are able to do most of the work and relax in the evening, so that you don't feel the need to sleep late at night.

Get into your work "state" after your daily grooming routine and slip into your work clothes at least half an hour before leaving for office and then sitting down to look at your MOD for the day and getting into an execution mode. Get the threads buzzing in the morning by focusing on your MOD plan for the day. Work to be executed must be loaded in your mind "RAM", ready to be executed.

The MOD ideally should be aligned to your energy rhythm and involves doing those thinking and creative tasks in the morning.

7.1.3 THE WORK DAY – ZONE OF PRODUCTIVITY / VALUE ADDITION

As a ground rule for playing this game, you have to execute what is scheduled. You have to start consulting your watch more often. Remember this is a new way to lead your life. It is a new template. But it is still on paper, it has to be habituated by your mind as a way of executing things first. You will find initially your master of the day lying by your side while you would be engaged but slowly you will pick it up more and more till it starts defining your new work routine. The trick lies in making yourself do it, till it becomes second nature and once you start tasting small victories, you will be hooked.

Execute the tasks, project threads and noise as planned. Perform the project threads and tasks completely as it gives you the insight and motivation to go to the next step. Apply productivity strategies to do all work in the most optimal way.

Noise will be one of the biggest factors that will have to be managed. Noise, as we saw earlier, is not just the small nagging tasks but also the thought, anxieties and worries that trouble you and keep you distracted. Thus, it is very important that you manage the physical and cerebral noise. But do remember one similarity; they all are residing in your mind and that is where they need to be tackled first.

Our life is so dynamic that despite our best planning, it would be impossible to do everything as per plan. These variances will have to accepted as part of your execution. During this time your productivity and focus are of prime importance. You must be in your state to execute and focus. Apply the productivity strategies religiously and don't let noise disturb you whatever may be the urge. If the tasks and threads are manageable within the day, then try to take them to completion. Remember the "Eat the Elephant" principle; Don't try to overachieve until and unless you have the deadline looming large. In that case, you may have to put aside your other tasks and projects.

For managing your day, the work priority and schedule must remain visible to you. What is visible to you and is active in your mind is what will get executed. Therefore, it is very important to keep revising, reminding yourself of about your main tasks, projects and goals for the day.

The key to coming out of the day is to switch to create

boundaries around the scheduled work. The tasks and threads you have deferred are still in the line of execution but you are the master here. It all might seem a bit daunting but when you have reason and passion to back up an endeavor, it happens.

7.1.4 YOUR NEW MASTER OF THE DAY SCHEDULE

Your new schedule could be looking like this as shown below. It may vary from person to person but it has to be made. It may look crowded or too much of an effort. But remember, that the scheduled tasks are your ticket to happiness, health, betterment, and richness.

The plan shown below is only indicative and may differ from person to person. There might not be time for personal projects on weekdays and may have to be scheduled on weekends. To keep the personal projects running you may have to delegate or hand it over to professionals. If you have a job, then the only time you may have is on weekends. You can plan to work on the project for a fixed time. While weekends are meant for relaxation, but that is the only time when your 9-5 is not blocked by your job or business.

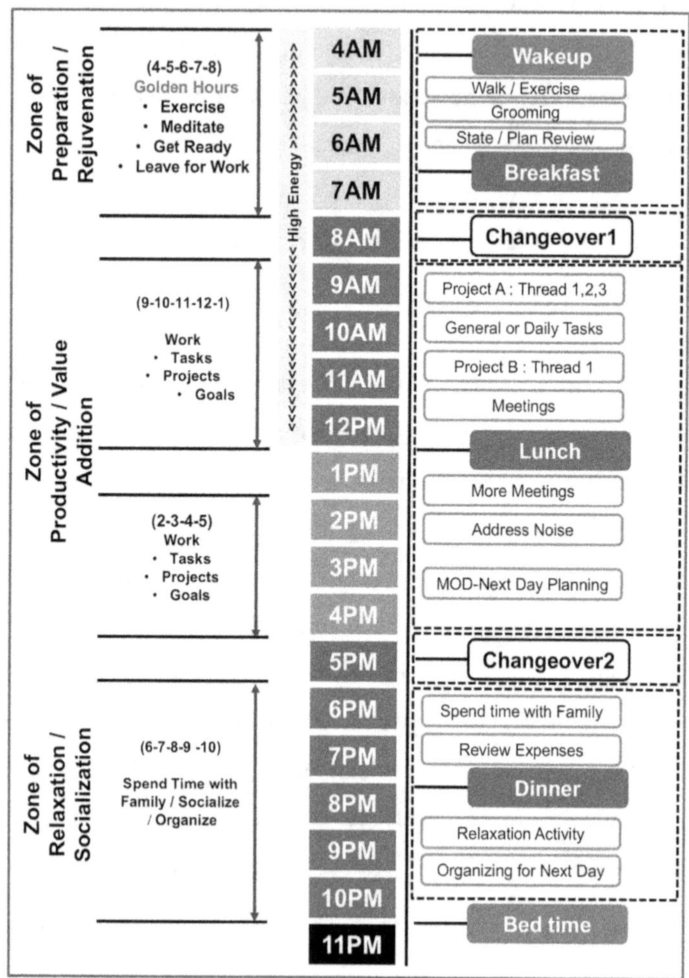

7.1.5 THE DAILY RULES

The following principles are enablers for following the Master of the Day framework. They will act as guides to help you get started and finish any type of work. Some of these are like hygiene factors which will ensure that you can quickly select, understand, execute and complete any type of work.

Respect the Daily Limits: The Daily Framework limits that you set for yourself are inviolable. Any new routine has to be built on a foundation of discipline, commitment, resolve, and a vision, else the routine will provide sub-optimal results or may fall away altogether.

You can't skimp on one aspect of the day and compensate for the other. Evenings and nights are easy targets for stretching our office work into and consume them. We justify this by saying that work can't wait or you will catch your sleep over the weekend. Bottom-line is that the Master of the Day *changeovers* are non-negotiable!

Review your Finances Daily: Money is one of the main reasons that we hesitate to make decisions especially those involving recreational expenses like taking a holiday or buying something expensive that will make you happy. By proper expense and budget management, you can cut out the anxiety involved in making sudden or big expenses. Start your day with a review of your expenses versus budget till date and you will be likely to splurge less. Plan for big expenses and avoid financing big expenses through debt. Expense and budget management will anchor all your money related decisions.

Budget Your Time: Life affords us an opportunity to make deposits to make our future better or give in to lure of the moment of gratification. On a daily basis, we have the option to spend two things, time and money. While we are very careful about spending money, we are not that careful about spending time. Learn to budget your time. Soon you will realize that you have all the time to work and also spend it on leisure activities without feeling guilty.

Keep a Review Log: The Review Log is an important artifact that will help you evolve your MOD approach day by day. In the next two-three weeks' time, you would have a fair idea of what is working and what has to be changed.

Balance is another key factor that leads to a wholesome consumption of the day and ensuring that you don't overlook important aspects of your life i.e. Health, Family, Money and Work. Needless to say not paying attention to anyone of these or related areas will sow the seeds for future issues and problems.

Keep Visualizing: Visualization is such a powerful tool that we all have but we hardly use it to our work situations. It can provide us all the answers that we are seeking.

Account for Variation Not all days will be equal; neither will be the tasks and the time they will take. Make provisions for variation in your routine for un-anticipated issues, events like travelling, sickness, traffic jams, sudden urgency. Also, you have to choose between quick gratification and achieving your goals. Life affords us an opportunity to make deposits to make our future better or keep spending time to seek gratification.

Have a Health Routine to have the energy and align your most important projects with the peak energy times when you are the most productive. It's better to waste your time in trying to achieve something rather than wasting time otherwise. Learn the lessons, change or keep on suffering.

7.2 WHAT IS YOUR DAY LOOKING LIKE NOW?

If you have reached this far then hopefully you would have spent a week or two with your new designer days. How did they go? What difference do you find? Did you find them too much to handle? Did you give up?

Well, you would have partial answers to all of the above questions, but it's natural. Like all the things in life we learnt, we have to give anything new a little time before it gets ingrained into our daily routine. Gains will come and may have already started coming. We are trying to balance our days per our value system, work type and against ingrained habits. It will take time. The trick is to keep repeating it. It's your own journey, you have identified the destination and also how best to get there. I have tried to give you a framework; you have to adapt it make it your own. The routine took me a while to get used to but it's part of my life now. All things that we start with are a bit rough and awkward. They get refined over a period of time. If you think adopting something new is difficult, then consider the following:

1. How do you drive the car now compared to when you just learnt?

2. The ease with which you are able to type on a keyboard compared to when you started.

Now let's see if the MOD framework has enabled us to use the levers mentioned earlier in Chapter 4.

1) Creating More Space

The "Day Framework" assigns definite structure and clearly demarcates your public and private space with inviolable changeover periods. This would have created space if you have started following the day structure. It also assigns you to follow definite sleep and waking up time to capture your day. The *Vital 4* elements if incorporated will ensure that you do a few things that lends balance to your day. This is the beginning of space creation as and when you want without losing track of your workload and completion targets.

The E-Framework allows you to work more productively and with agility. Both the Frameworks work together with one, defining daily limits and ensuring that the imposition of limits forces you to plan and finish planned activities on time. The other, creates a process to handle work effectively, eliminating noise, starting potential and all the effectiveness destroyers.

2) Understanding and Executing our Priorities

The Day Framework again is the first framework, which puts some critical priorities in place like sleeping and waking up on time, making time for family and self. The E-Framework ensures that you have a two-step process to validate incoming work viz. Initial screening under List / Categorize and Prioritization of work under the Choice element. The MOD Framework will make you more self-aware of how to understand, select and execute priorities.

3) Isolating Signal from the Noise that Surrounds Us

Noise is completely controlled and if you have started taking pro-active steps the various elements of noise as described in Chapter 3 are now being addressed proactively and strategically. You would have developed working mechanisms for managing noise and eliminated cerebral noise by stopping to ruminate endlessly on inane worries which basically you have conjured out of nothing and keep agonising over. Based on the methodology and strategies for managing noise you are now able to isolate all forms of noise and take effective measures to minimize or eliminate it. At the same time working on your priorities ensures that your "Signal" tasks become stronger and better.

4) Becoming Productive

You are able to work much more productively having the constraint of getting up from work at the change over time in the evening. With the productivity methodology / strategies outlined, you are able to finish work using optimal techniques which are shorn of wastes. Decision making should much easier to you now. You know to get work done you have to make decisions. You are much more at ease with the decision methodology and have adapted it to your own specific needs. The work that you do begin with a decision backing it up so there is very little stress.

As you begin planning and have right-sized work filling up exact schedules in which they can be finished, you start getting more done. Limiting the number of work items that you have lined up during the day means that you are able to achieve more and with lesser stress. Having the enablement framework ensures that you understand the importance of elements like organization, clarity, scheduling, focus and state.

5) Becoming Proactive

Proactive means to be able to view work lined up in the near future and acting upon it in advance. It also is about taking time before we plunge headlong into a project or task. This act can actually let us know what we are getting into and also estimate the pitfalls and the time it will take. This really liberates you and creates the space that you crave for. The Daily, Weekly, Monthly, Yearly planning that MOD advocates gives you a ringside view of what lies in store in the near future and what constraints, bottlenecks lie along the way. The E-Framework works to help clarify the projects and tasks you have undertaken to get them done more efficiently and effectively.

6) Creating Balance

The MOD Framework comprehensively introduces the concept of balance by laying stress on following daily routine prescribed by the Day Framework which makes space for self, family, relation and friends. At the same time, this is bolstered by the "Vital 4" categories which prescribe picking at least one activity out of each of the four vital categories. Each activity takes very less time and can easily be done anytime during the day.

7.3 THE MOD CHECKLIST

Checklists are a great way to ensure all the key tasks are performed and nothing is skipped. The MOD Checklist given below is a quick and ready reckoner to check if you are going through the motions. It works great when you are still to fully get into the MOD routine and forget the vital steps.

MOD Planning for the Day

1. How did the day go? How many scheduled tasks / projects were you able to complete?
2. Did you honor your MOD schedule once prepared?
3. Did you prepare the MOD plan for the next day?
4. Did you refer to the Weekly and Monthly schedule?

List / Categorize

1. Did you capture the tasks as and when they came to your notice?
2. Did all the work that you captured was screened?

Choice

1. Did you use the prioritisation approaches to identify key tasks for the next day?

Decision

1. Did you take the important decisions related to the tasks / project threads?

Clarify

1. Did you thread the projects? Are the threads specific and progressive?

Organize

1. Did you set-up the tasks/project threads for the next day?
2. Did you organize your stuff (in your computer or work place) before leaving?

Schedule

1. Are the top tasks scheduled as identified during prioritization?
2. Are the tasks/threads aligned with your productivity curve?
3. Have you organized specific value added activities from the "Vital 4" categories?

State

1. Did you enter the state before focusing on the tasks of the Day?

Focus

1. Did you review your work plan and also the tasks lined up?
2. Did you begin with some tasks to get your focus?

Productivity

1. Did you apply productivity strategies to optimise your work?
2. Were you able to stick to "Power of One" by finishing the top tasks one by one?

Sustain

1. Did you create deadlines?
2. Did you work out strategies to prevent the pace from flagging?

Complete

1. Were you able to take your task/ project threads to completion?
2. Did your work reach the climax stage?
3. Did you have to work diligently sacrificing all distractions before the work got completed?
4. Did you ship your work output?

Evolve

1. Did you think beyond completion and take your completed work beyond the set boundaries?

Remember the day when you accomplished something big a lot of things happened you were in a zone, you felt light, happier as if a load has been taken off your load. But just before the work got accomplished, there was frantic activity all around. There was only a limited amount of energy, time, and focus to spend on life and as such we should apply it to the biggest priorities and take action. Your MOD routine will help you achieve all this and much more!

In the next and final chapter, we look at some of the final pieces which will help you in sustaining the Master of the Day regime. We will look at the derailment factors which can off-track your pursuit to master your day. The Master of the Day Maturity Levels gives you a measurable criteria and scale to track your progress. Finally, we come to the vision of the Master of the Day i.e. to become ready for the coming future when machines will take over much of the work we are currently doing.

THE EVOLUTION

Master of the Day Epilogue

"Live as if you were to die tomorrow.
Learn as if you were to live forever"
Mahatma Gandhi

8.1 THE BLUEPRINT FOR YOUR SUCCESS

We have reached the last chapter of this book, but perhaps for you the journey has just begun. Leading a better and more meaningful life is about doing things a little better every time. It's about adding and improving what is already working for you.

Guys, change can begin anytime, maybe the entire book before this didn't sound like a reason enough and maybe one event can trigger that urge in you to become better. If things don't seem to be working so far, then also hang on. Our life is governed by something called as destiny. Destiny brings changes when we least expect it. It might as well be destiny at work if you found this book as impractical and one day you might again pick it up and go all the way and adopt it wholeheartedly.

It may just be a medium to take you towards what you desire and have been aspiring for years. If things are still not working, the magic in you remains somnambulant, and then perhaps you need to tweak things here and there. You are unique, your aura and destiny have only one unique imprint in the universe. If you have decided to get up and start taking control of your life then maybe it just your destiny that is making you do all those things. You have to create your own story guided by your destiny.

Mohandas Karamchand Gandhi, whom the world knows as the apostle of non-violence and as the Father of the Indian nation was a man who adopted a persona and a daily routine to keep up with his mission to gain freedom for India from the British through non-violent means. When a human being is on a mission, everything falls into place. He or she gets transformed to bring that change. Thus, Gandhi once said, "Be the change that you wish to see in the world." He saw poverty all around and thus gave up on his western lifestyle and adopted the attire of the masses.

Thus he went down to minimalist needs to sustain his day to day living in tune with his mission. In the name of covering himself, he just wore a simple dhoti (a cotton garment) spun by himself. This went by his call to shun clothes produced in Britain. Apart from this, he ate frugal meals during the day. The rest of his day was spent meeting a constant stream of visitors through the day and answering mounds of letters that he received daily.

The only material possession of any value that he had was a pocket watch which he consulted first thing in the morning at 4:00 AM and then often during the day. He was known for his legendary punctuality. Without a time management routine, he would never have been able to accomplish what he did during the day. He also understood clearly that living this way demands a certain mindset and thus he once disclosed that, "The concept of changing yourself, to reflect what you want to see around you is simple in theory but require hard work, patience, and determination to attain". Despite all his engagements, Mahatma Gandhi never turned away anyone saying he is overly busy. He was able to create space as and when he wanted. This can only be done by a person who has planned but kept margin and flexibility to use his disposable time without losing track and adherence to the main tasks of the day.

Similarly, you have to devise your own Master of the Day schedule. The one that will fulfill all your wishes, keeps you in control and leads you to a life of eternal happiness. If you are unable to do so, just imagine what an ideal day will look like with you going through your very own MOD routine. What are your feelings? Do you feel more relaxed and confident as you see yourself doing things that you always wanted to do? It all depends on you!

Master of the Day is nothing but taking over of what is truly your life. Somewhere in the rigmarole of life, this time control has been hijacked by trivia, commitments, making a living, pressures and finally a lack of space to rethink the script. Tomorrow is too far and too uncertain. On top of that what you do today will determine what you do tomorrow.

8.2 THE DERAILMENT FACTORS

An elaborate methodology requires patience and determination. There will be many pitfalls and challenges which will frustrate and deter you. The derailment factors is a listing of some of these factors which you will have to grapple with constantly before the MOD becomes a part of your life.

Not sleeping on time: This is one key activity around which MOD is pivoted. You miss this and you will have to compensate by extra sleep in your golden hours. Not sleeping on time will have an effect on you throughout your day. Thus, lack of timely and quality sleep is the first requisite for executing as per the Master of the Day routine.

Not preparing the plan a day before: The plan for the next day must be ready a day before. This is the time to review how your day has gone; tasks, projects; noise and other tasks lined up for tomorrow and do the scheduling accordingly.

General or unspecific threads: For project threads to be effective they must be specific and actionable and with a fair assessment of how much time they would take. Nonspecific or informational threads will be unclear and specific action cannot be taken. Your most important projects and goals must have crisp and action-oriented threads. After a thread is executed, it's a good practice to keep notes and next action steps that may emerge from them.

Decisions not taken a day before: You can't mix decisions and action together; they require totally different approaches and state of mind. Decisions can choke you and won't even get you started. At the root of procrastination lies indecision.

Not having a vision for the day: What exactly will you do today? A vision will drive things invisibly. No amount of words can replace a mental picture. Hence visualization as a technique is a constant aid that you use to peer into what you want to become or want to achieve. A vision will make the day special or even magically drive you while a lack of one will make the day seem like an ordinary one.

Not aligning with your productivity curve: We all have our most productive times when we are at our productive best. Productivity dips as our body begins to tire during the day. Not doing the most creative tasks at times when you are your most productive and fresh is letting go of a period when a lot of your issues and work would find much better solutions

Not honoring your MOD schedule once prepared: Once a schedule has been made, it has to be executed. It's your own commitment to yourself and to your family for a better tomorrow.

Having a multi-focus: Trying to do too many things or multitasking is a sign of disaster and an indicator that you are anxious. Have faith in yourself and also have mercy on your wonderful brain. It's eager to serve you but give it many tasks to go for at once and it will begin to crawl and start looking for escape routes. Multitasking is a bad way of execution, it might give you the satisfaction that you are getting more done, but at the end of it you will have nothing to show against your efforts. It's a classic case of going against the E-Framework and gets nothing done. Work in Progress must be as less as possible to ensure that you achieve your objectives and priorities.

Work not captured when it occurs: Your mind is constantly active and your consciousness is already bombarded with opportunities, thoughts, reminders, and situations which require you to respond at a later time. But just like computer RAM, it does not stay there and before you know, the work is forgotten. Having a reliable process for capturing all your incoming work is the first step to getting them done. Even small tasks if left undone can boil over and topple your best laid plans for the day.

Not reviewing or monitoring your progress: Failure to review will be a recipe for your effort to become the Master of the Day to stutter and ultimately fail. Daily and weekly review must accompany daily planning to keep your MOD plan on track.

8.3 MASTER OF THE DAY MATURITY LEVELS

No one becomes a champion overnight. Anyone who has achieved anything significant had to toil maybe for years together away from the limelight, away from the normal life that majority of us leads. Master of the Day is a complete transformation program. It won't happen overnight. However, the more it is adopted, the more it will start giving benefits. The entire methodology is subjected to the same value destroyers that we have come across throughout the book. Thus, it is recommended to latch onto this new way of living in a realistic and time bound manner. Based upon personal experience, the following levels are meant to serve as a guide to slowly becoming more and more adept at the methodology. The period mentioned is indicative and may vary from person to person.

Level 1: The Beginning – This is the first stage of awareness that some structure has to be put around your day and work has to be listed, prioritised and executed properly. You have understood the need for doing MOD and are exploring it as a means to solve your daily routine. At this stage you struggle with Day Framework and are not regular with your use of the E-Framework but are still trying to settle into a rudimentary MOD routine. However, you start maintaining a basic work list, do some prioritisation and become aware of the various zones of the day. You might take 1-3 months to complete Level 1.

Level 2: The Enforcement – At this stage, you will start realising that this kind of routine is hard to implement. Even a small change in your routine takes a lot of time, but you have now the urge to follow the guidelines and hence are more determined. Thus, you start enforcing the routine more rigidly. Your Day Framework will be the first thing to fall into place. You might spend 3-6 months to complete Level 2.

Level 3: Settlement – This is the stage when the MOD routine i.e. Daily Framework and E-Framework starts happening almost daily. There are still days when things don't go as planned but you are able to predict and take corrective actions. This might take you 6-8 months to achieve.

Level 4: Regularisation – This is the stage when you have made the Day Framework and E-Framework process a part of your daily routine. Regularity also helps you to build the pace. You are now working on your goals almost daily and this makes you much happier and of course better. This level might take you 8-12 months.

Level 5: Evolution - This is the stage when you have made the Day Framework and E-Framework your second nature. You have overcome most of the major derailment factors and are also able to handle variations in your daily routine. You will at this stage start evolving the model to better meet your requirements. This would typically take 12-18 month when you have ironed out most of the issues surrounding your routine and its evolution.

MASTER PRACTITIONER

This is the stage when you decide to move beyond MOD. You have made MOD a way of life and has imbibed its principles. All complex things move towards simplicity. Work is not an end but only a means to an end. MOD will then merge into the background as if on an autopilot. You are a like a car racing driver driving on city roads. There is no stress and you seek the deeper meaning of work and life. Your life is now organized and you can take the call that if you quit a regular routine and pursue some higher path. Master Practitioner phase has no beginning or an end but will not be before completion of at least 18 month of MOD adoption.

The Maturity levels at a summary level are depicted below.

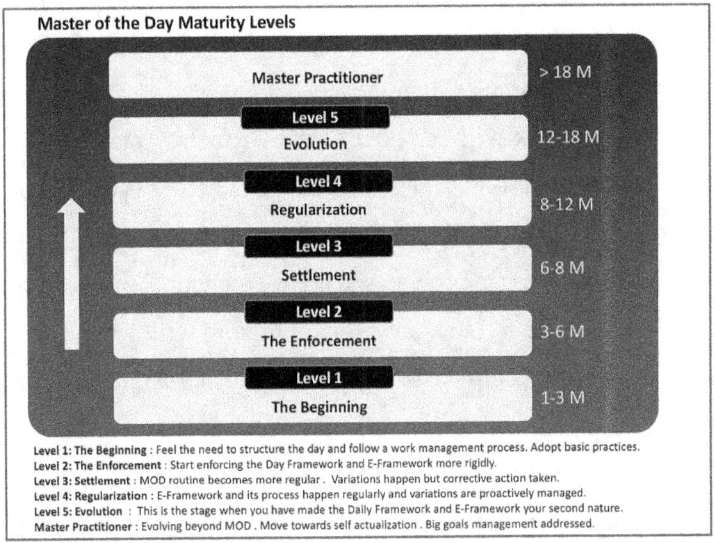

8.4 MASTER OF THE DAY IN NEAR FUTURE

The transformation for an intelligent human race has started. This is an age bubbling right in the cusp of a disruption we are in. Technology is going to alter the world. Human Excellence will be the new denominator of success. At the same time, technology will drive the new world. Very soon what we started watching and reading in movies and books will materialize before our eyes. Robots will be omnipresent, personal flying objects will soon fill the skies and a new race of intelligent human race will rapidly create a new virtually enabled world order where no countries exist. The next few years will see the creation of virtual online assets, virtual reality enabled life experiences and stuff we could not even visualize just a couple of decades back. Human excellence which hitherto resided within precincts of big institutions and corporates has no specific coordinates now. Start-ups can erupt anywhere and individuals can create personal instances of excellence and creativity and announce it online.

Common work will be taken over by robots. This leaves us with real brainy stuff to deal with. The age of heroes is over. From now on everyone is enabled to become a hero. You have all the knowledge with you to become and know anything. However, how soon you are able to latch onto something big will depend upon how you are able to utilize make your intelligence available during the day. You can see it everywhere. All the bottled up creativity,

entrepreneurship and intelligence of the masses is coming out whether in the form of start-ups, you-tube channels or even in the form of harmless fun-filled WhatsApp videos.

As company structures break, a company will be a quasi-static-cluster of consenting free agents who come together for a contracted period providing desired outputs, collaborating with other group resources, holding web meetings. In short, all the work that happens in an organization will be virtually delivered and no dedicated work-force working in the 9-5 regime. The day of the free agents is here!

While some conventional structure will remain but most of the task force deployed will be an ethereal mass of humanity pervading the internet. Master of the day is a book written in the cusp of a change. For us to be ready for the change, we have to unravel the intelligence that lies within us. For this, we have to become more productive, methodical and ruthlessly guard what will be the most premium commodity on earth i.e. Time. With, no guarantee of a fixed salary, you have to bring out your "A" game every day as you are in business.

Friends this is it! It's over to you. Write your own story. Before I sign off and hand it over to you remember to not forget the one principle that we discussed earlier: "Eat the Elephant". The task before you is nothing less than an elephant but if you persevere, and take things gradually, you will surely find success. I have tried to address the entire spectrum of issues surrounding our daily life and shown the way the MOD can help manage it better. However, this book is an inert piece of paper until you bring it to life. No one will come and programme it into you. You are the software and hardware and you are the programmer, all rolled into one. Take the leap of faith and try it once. It might just make you achieve your wildest dreams or at a modest level, it might make your life slightly better, healthier, happier and richer. Either way, you are a winner!!

"Death is nothing, but to live defeated and inglorious is to die daily"
Napoleon Bonaparte

Annexure – MOD Templates

9.1 MASTER OF THE DAY TEMPLATE

This is the actual Master of the Day Template which you may use to plan your day. This is just an illustration; you may use your diary planner, phone / laptop to plan and schedule your tasks and project threads.

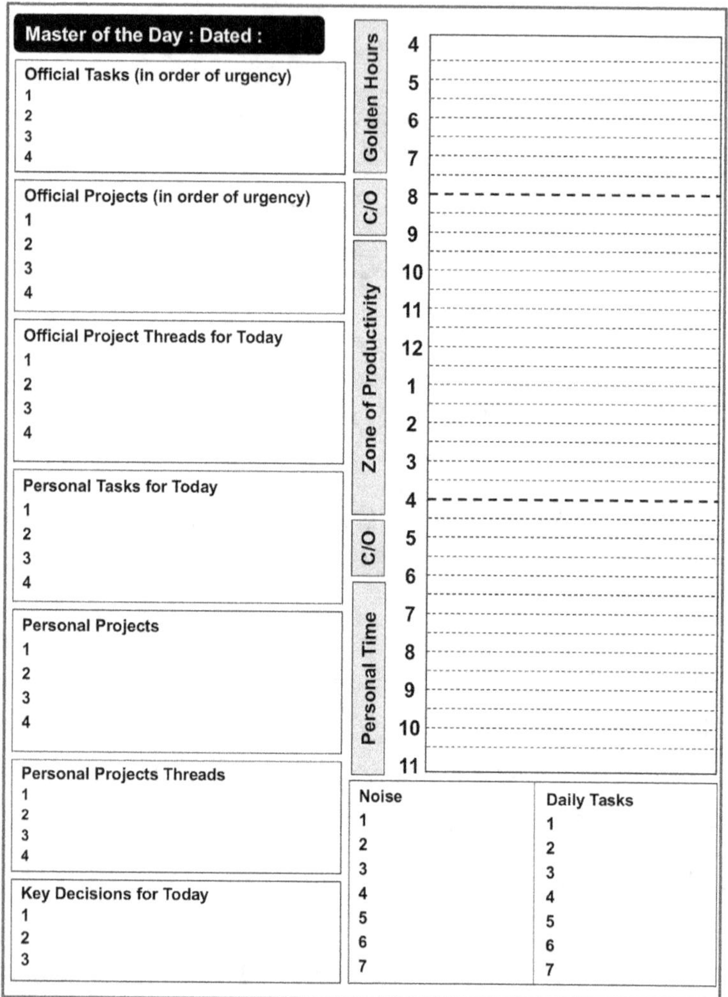

Master of the Day : Dated :
Official Tasks (in order of urgency)
1
2
3
4
Official Projects (in order of urgency)
1
2
3
4
Official Project Threads for Today
1
2
3
4
Personal Tasks for Today
1
2
3
4
Personal Projects
1
2
3
4
Personal Projects Threads
1
2
3
4
Key Decisions for Today
1
2
3
Golden Hours
C/O
Zone of Productivity
C/O
Personal Time
4
5
6
7
8
9
10
11
12
1
2
3
4
5
6
7
8
9
10
11
Noise
1
2
3
4
5
6
7
Daily Tasks
1
2
3
4
5
6
7

9.2 PROJECT AND TASKS LIST

The Template below is the listing of Projects and Tasks together. The Projects information will not change frequently but Tasks will keep changing. There will be in addition to Incoming Tasks, Daily Tasks which have to be done daily. This includes attending to bio- needs, exercise, grooming, commuting, maintaining expenses, MOD planning. The Daily Tasks may vary from person to person.

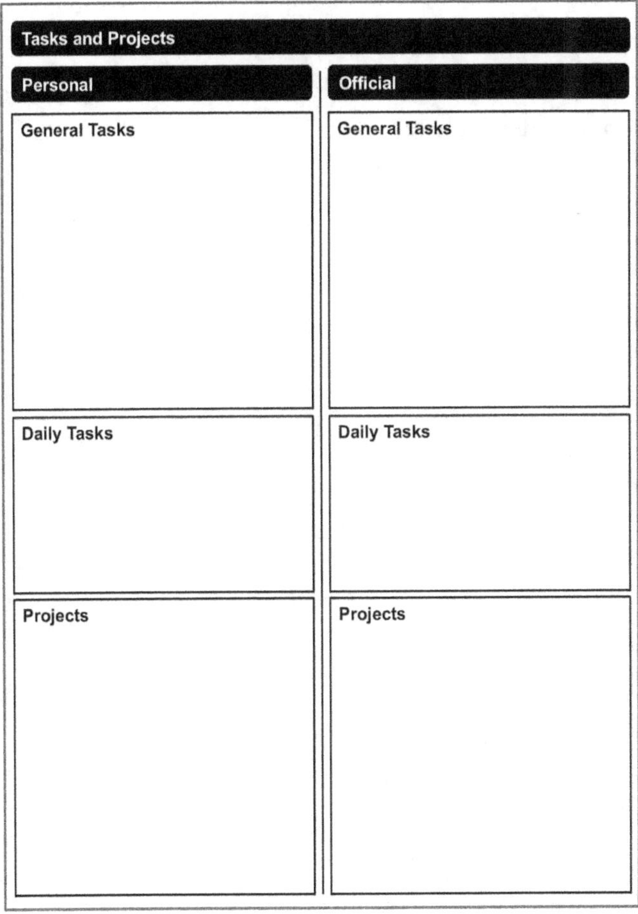

9.3 NOISE

Noise template will help you to list down the noise in your life and help cluster and manage it better so you can minimise or tackle the noise tasks better on a daily basis and focus on your core tasks.

Compile a list of noise issues you face. Chances are there is a pattern. Only 20% of the Noise Factors are causing you issues. Eliminating them will solve 80% of your issues.

On a daily basis, if you can identify what is bothering you and what are the activities which would be urgent but not exactly life changing, then you can isolate and dispose of these activities much more effectively.

Noise	
Task Related	**People**
Cerebral	**Environment**

9.4 PROJECT THREADS

The following template will provide an indication of first level threading of projects. You may however like to elaborate on this by adding more columns like duration of each thread, responsibility, starting and end date etc.

Project Threads (Measurable, Achievable ,Progressive, Specific)	
Official / Business	**Personal**
Project 1 Thread 1 Thread 2 Thread 3 Thread 4 Thread 5 Thread 6 Thread 7 Thread 8 Thread 9 Thread 10	**Project 1** Thread 1 Thread 2 Thread 3 Thread 4 Thread 5 Thread 6 Thread 7 Thread 8 Thread 9 Thread 10
Project 2 Thread 1 Thread 2 Thread 3 Thread 4 Thread 5 Thread 6 Thread 7 Thread 8 Thread 9 Thread 10	**Project 2** Thread 1 Thread 2 Thread 3 Thread 4 Thread 5 Thread 6 Thread 7 Thread 8 Thread 9 Thread 10
Project 3 Thread 1 Thread 2 Thread 3 Thread 4 Thread 5 Thread 6 Thread 7 Thread 8 Thread 9 Thread 10	**Project 3** Thread 1 Thread 2 Thread 3 Thread 4 Thread 5 Thread 6 Thread 7 Thread 8 Thread 9 Thread 10

9.5 WEEKLY TEMPLATE

The following templates will help visualise how forthcoming week looks like. This is absolutely vital as the MOD provides a sharp focus on the present day. The weekly view provides a head's up on what's lined up and how it will have to be factored in your MOD for the days to come. You can take a printout or create this weekly schedule in MS Office applications. You may also alternatively use the scheduler's apps on your smartphone or laptop.

Week Plan – High Level Tasks / Projects		
Day 1	**Day 2**	**Day 3**
Day 4	**Day 5**	**Day 6**
Day 7		

Used for deciding major tasks / activities

This is a Weekly Scheduler having the hourly schedule visible across at a weekly level. Again depending upon preference you can maintain this on a printout of this template, a planner diary, spread sheet/presentation/document

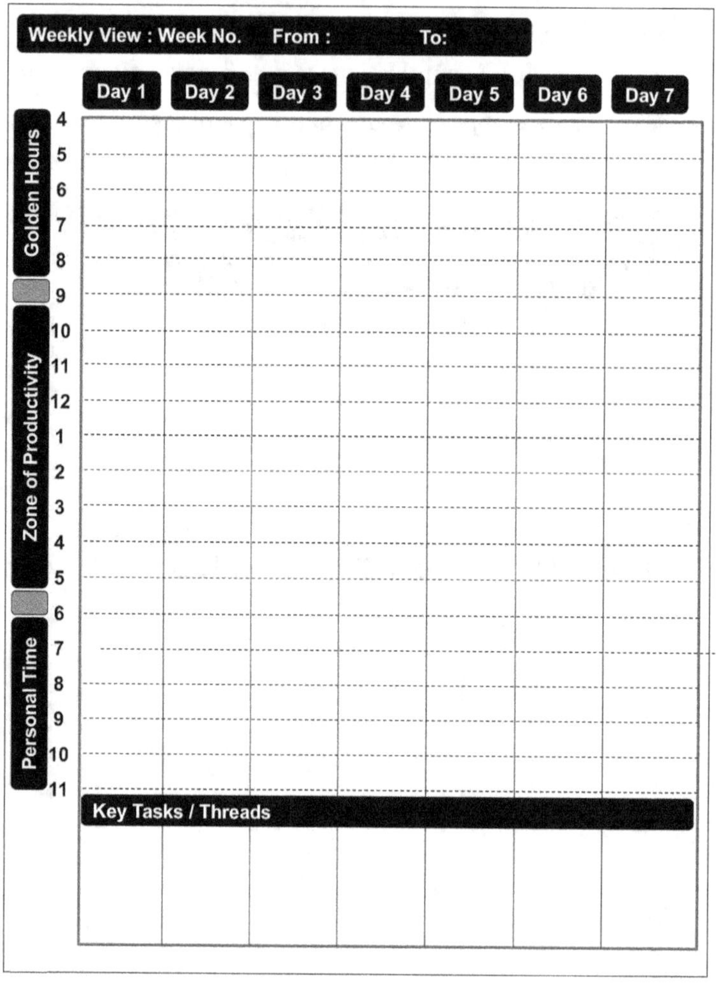

9.6 MONTHLY VIEW

The monthly view provides a longer perspective than a week and helps you place the major work for each day.

Month View

Day 1	Day 2	Day 3	Day 4	Day 5
Day 6	Day 7	Day 8	Day 9	Day 10
Day 11	Day 12	Day 13	Day 14	Day 15
Day 16	Day 17	Day 18	Day 19	Day 20
Day 21	Day 22	Day 23	Day 24	Day 25
Day 26	Day 27	Day 28	Day 29	Day 30
Day 31				

9.7 YEAR VIEW

The Year view provides a yearly perspective and provides a "Helicopter Vision" of important events dates, work lined up at a high level during the current year.

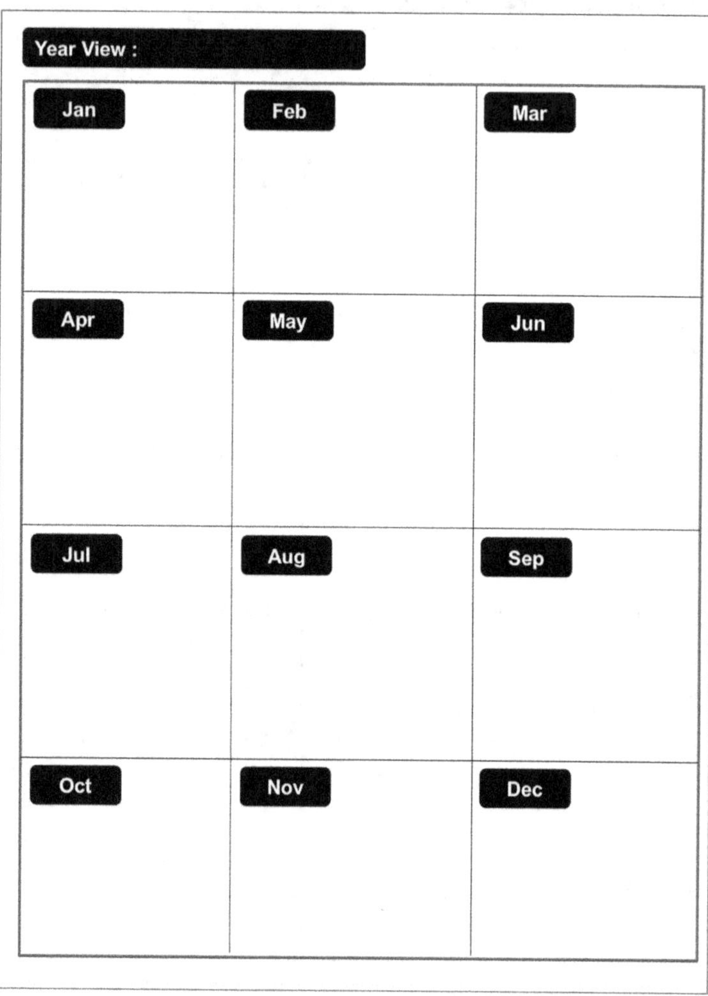

Bibliography

Page 35, How do we spend the day? Section 2.3 Where does your time go? Source: National Sleep Foundation, Sleep Times https://www.sleepfoundation.org/press-release/ national-sleep-foundation-recommends-new-sleep-times

P 49, Making it all Work within a Day, Section 3.1.2 Strategies. Source: Benjamin Franklin Quote on 5 Why Analysis appeared in his journal, The Poor Richard's Almanac in 1758. The actual origins of this quote remains contested and it seems to have been adapted, modified over several centuries.

Page 141, E-Framework – Selection & Understanding, Section 5.4 Decision - Benjamin Franklin Pros and Cons method; Source: Benjamin Franklin, Mr. Franklin: A Selection from His Personal Letters, 1956.

Page 23, A Day to do it, Section 1.5 The Need to become the Master of the Day. Iroha is an old poem said to have been written by Kukai (774~835), who was a famous Japanese monk in the early (Heian Era 794~1185. An English translation by Professor Ryuichi Abe).

Page 107-109, Making it all Happen within a Day, Section 4.4 Day Framework. Benjamin Franklin Case Study inspired by his time/

self-management practices which appeared in the "The Autobiography of Benjamin Franklin".

Page 198, Master of the Day Epilogue, Section 8.1 the Blueprint for Your Success, Mahatma Gandhi Case Study inspired by his time management practices in the "The Autobiography of Mahatma Gandhi": "The Story of my Experiments with Truth" by M.K. Gandhi.